YOUR KNOWLEDGE

- We will publish your bachelor's and master's thesis, essays and papers

- Your own eBook and book - sold worldwide in all relevant shops

- Earn money with each sale

Upload your text at www.GRIN.com
and publish for free

Bibliographic information published by the German National Library:

The German National Library lists this publication in the National Bibliography;
detailed bibliographic data are available on the Internet at http://dnb.dnb.de .

Imprint:

Copyright © 2012 GRIN Verlag, Open Publishing GmbH
Print and binding: Books on Demand GmbH, Norderstedt Germany
ISBN: 978-3-668-17181-7

This book at GRIN:

http://www.grin.com/en/e-book/317922/walknavi-augmented-reality-navigation-
and-reminder-system-for-people-with

Eldar Mammadli

WalkNavi. Augmented-Reality Navigation and Reminder System for People with Mild Dementia

GRIN Publishing

GRIN - Your knowledge has value

Since its foundation in 1998, GRIN has specialized in publishing academic texts by students, college teachers and other academics as e-book and printed book. The website www.grin.com is an ideal platform for presenting term papers, final papers, scientific essays, dissertations and specialist books.

Visit us on the internet:

http://www.grin.com/

http://www.facebook.com/grincom

http://www.twitter.com/grin_com

Contents

List of Figures

List of Tables

List of abbreviations

ADF	Automatic Direction Finder
aGPS	assisted GPS
AMi	Alzheimer Monitoring
AR	Augmented Reality
ARNS	Augmented Reality Navigation System
CAC	Call Admission Control
CDMA	Code Division Multiple Access
EGNOS	European Geostationary Navigation Overlay Service
ENABLE	Enabling Technologies for People with Dementia
EU	European Union
HMD	Head-Mounted Display
IRNSS	Indian Regional Navigation Satellite System
Invw	Interview
InPa	Interviewee
ITU	International Telecommunication Union
GLONASS	Global Navigation Satellite System
GPS	Global Positioning System
GSM	Global System for Mobile Communications
STM	Short-Term Memory
LED	Light-Emitting Diod
MSAS	Multi-functional Satellite Augmentation System
NAVSTAR	Navigational Satellite Timing and Ranging
POI	Point of Interest
RaDaR	Radio Detection and Ranging
SDP	Session Description Protocol
SIP	Session Initiation Protocol
TCP	Transmission Control Protocol

TED	Technology, Ethics and Dementia
TLS	Transport Layer Security
UDP	User Datagram Protocol
URI	Uniform Resource Indicator
VDF	VHF Direction Finder
VHF	Very High Frequency
VoIP	Voice over Internet Protocol
WAAS	Wide Area Augmentation System
WLAN	Wireless Local Area Network

„I fear I am not in my perfect mind.

Methinks I should know you, and know this man;

Yet I am doubtful for I am mainly ignorant

What place this is; and all the skill I have

Remembers not these garments; nor I know not

Where I did lodge last night. Do not laugh at me."

The Tragedy of King Lear (VII), William Shakespeare

1. Introduction

The fundamental idea of this study is to investigate problems faced by people with mild dementia in terms of disorientation, and to be able to analyse options for support in terms of navigation. Based on this information, a navigation system is to be developed that helps people with dementia in the early stages to overcome spatial and temporal orientation problems. The system should be controlled remotely by the caregiver, and where possible, fulfil the sufferer's requirement of being simple to operate. The task of this study is then to identify the particular requirements of dementia sufferers that in principle set them apart from other target groups. These can be questions of privacy, but also societal, personal and illness-specific aspects. The following chapters will provide more details on these questions. When we speak of dementia, the role of supporting sufferers is also extremely important. Consequently, the system should also offer options for the caregiver to assist the affected person in an emergency situation. Besides the sufferer's coordination data, speech and video data are also transmitted to the caregiver, making it easier for him to locate and help the sufferer. In this regard, it is also important to establish the opinion of the sufferer in terms of monitoring, so that his privacy is not impinged upon. The primary target group of this study is people suffering from the early stages of dementia who are still capable of performing various tasks themselves. However, in addition to dementia sufferers, the system should also be able to be used by people with poor short-term memory (STM) whose memory has been damaged by an accident, for example. As a result, the design, and motivation of the study is explained, the most important reasons for choice of topic are listed, and the research questions identified and analysed. The chapter concludes with a discussion of the methodology used.

1.1. Design of the study

This study consists of seven main chapters. Figure 1.1 shows the method used in this study before treatment. For the implementation of the idea, the topic is approached by means of an analysis of the current state of research. The preliminary study augments the knowledge in this field. Information derived from the field of research and the preliminary study is identified in terms of the requirements, and the technologies and technical options needed for the implementation of these requirements are demonstrated. After implementation, the functionalities and possible technical shortcomings of the system are explained in detail. These deficiencies are identified again in the evaluation, which is performed with the dementia sufferers.

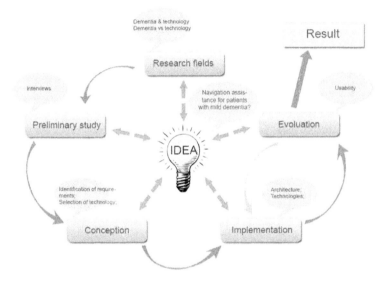

Figure 1.1.: Design of the study

The sub-chapter Motivation describes the idea of the study and presents its focus. This chapter contains basic information regarding the selection of topic. The problem is explained, and global trends regarding the ageing process and resultant illnesses, as well as new technical opportunities for problem resolution that can be expected in the future, are discussed. This chapter closes with a discussion on the methodology used for gathering information. Theoretical aspects of dementia are outlined in chapter 2. In addition, the stages of the illness are discussed, and the symptoms and consequences of the illness at each stage are explained. The following sub-chapter provides an overview of the current state of research. Examples of the implementation of technology in the care of dementia sufferers, and the technical support in general of these persons are the topics of the sub-chapter. The following chapter shows the results of the preliminary study, which had the aim of providing a better understanding of problems in dementia to be able to adequately identify the requirements that are significant for the application to be implemented. In addition, the difficulties faced by dementia sufferers are described; these relate to location and society, but are also of a personal nature. After determining the requirements of the application, chapter 4 explains the state of technology and provides a motivation for the technologies that were selected for fulfilment of the requirements from the research field and the preliminary study. In this regard, technologies and services such as Augmented Reality (AR), Voice over IP (VoIP) and Google Maps are examined more closely, the selection of technology is described in more detail and the selection criteria are formulated. Advantages and disadvantages are listed for each individual technology. The functionality and mode of operation of the system implemented are described in chapter 5. The analysis of the requirements that were realised and those that were not realised is also explained in this chapter. Suggestions for improvement and a solution are discussed briefly. The methodology used and the results of the evaluation are described in the chapter on evaluation. The detailed list of the shortcomings and the functions that are viewed by the affected persons as beneficial is also a topic of this chapter. Finally, suggestions for a solution are proposed. The last chapter summarises the results of this study and the contribution to research. To this end, the aspects of the research questions that could be answered are highlighted.

1.2. Motivation

The main aim of this study is to examine how modern technology can assist people with dementia and their relatives or caregivers in everyday life. In this regard, people with orientation problems are considered to be the target group. These individuals could be those suffering from the early stages of dementia as well as others with memory and orientation problems. Rapid advances in IT offer new options in all areas of life. New technologies alleviate problems experienced by people and often perform functions for them. Since the turn of the last century, mobile phones have practically become a self-evident part of almost everyone's life everywhere in the world, for example. Where mobile telephones were earlier used a means for verbal communication only, the development of the mobile internet, new devices and the appropriate software have meant that today they have almost all the functionality of a normal PC. Despite weaknesses like computing power, battery problems or the limited screen size, mobile phones have the significant advantage of mobility. This mobility opens many doors for use in different areas of life, and phone manufacturers are attempting to exploit the mobility of this device even further. This characteristic was a stimulus for manufacturers of mobile phones to make available functions that would not be useful for normal PCs. Examples of this are an integrated GPS receiver or a compass function. The existence of a GPS receiver enables the mobile phone to function as a navigation device. Besides the classic vehicle and aircraft navigation systems, pedestrian navigation systems are becoming increasingly popular. These systems are largely designed for tourists, although people with orientation problems can also benefit from them. People are reaching an advanced age ever more frequently, which in many cases leads to dementia. The older individuals become, the higher the incidence of dementia becomes.[1] Dementia means a constantly deteriorating memory. In advanced dementia, people suffer from increasing disorientation. Orientation difficulties occur initially at unfamiliar locations, and then later also at known locations.[2] Mobile pedestrian navigation systems can assist people suffering from dementia in this regard. Continuous support and care duties increase permanently.[3]

The pedestrian navigation system should be as simple and intuitive as possible, as dementia sufferers usually are of an advanced age and have poor STM. Augmented Reality (AR) technology is a visual technology that can alleviate this task. AR is used in many areas of industry, production or entertainment, and combines the real world with a virtual world in real time,

---

[1] Weissenberger, M. (2009) p. 10
[2] Gatterer, G. (2005) p. 18
[3] [Web/AZK]

presenting the result in 3D. The development of increased computing power and features for mobile phones ensures that the AR navigation systems are kept up to date. Various mobile phone applications are available today that support orientation at unfamiliar locations using AR technology. In this study, I will also attempt to answer questions as to whether AR technology offers options for dementia sufferers as well. Dementia patients require supportive assistance; they can land up in problematic situations from which they are unable to extract themselves on their own. To prevent difficulties of this nature, it would be useful for a caregiver to be able to provide support by remote monitoring. The problem of remote support is that caregivers are unable to place themselves in another person's situation. By using a combination of data from modern mobile phones and individual services, it is also possible for remote caregivers to display the location of the other person in real time. In addition, other information can be made available to the caregiver to assist in their assessment. The following chapters will detail what data and what technologies are required for this. This form of monitoring and support can also be used in other systems.

1.3. Methodology

The following section describes the methods and theories used in practice for the implementation of the application, and its evaluation. After the research questions regarding the state of research have been formulated in this chapter, interviews are conducted with the affected persons and their caregivers or relatives. As dementia occurs at an advanced age in most cases, respondents have only an extremely limited understanding of technology. In many cases, elderly people are not familiar with PCs or modern mobile phones. For this reason, questions can most probably not be answered in a structured interview. Consequently, a semi-structured[4] interview was selected. Learning is even more complicated for older persons suffering from dementia due to their poor STM. Besides the problem of age, other societal aspects emanate from the illness, such as lack of acceptance of the illness. The empirical data was evaluated based on the Grounded Theory process. This theory was developed by Anselm Strauss together with Barney Glaser, and is used for systematic evaluation of qualitative data in particular, with the goal of generating a theory. This theory generation from empirical data means that most hypotheses and concepts arise not from the data itself, but rather in the course of research.[5]

For this development, experimental prototyping is selected. A prototype is developed that meets all realisable requirements specified from the preliminary study. This process is selected with the aim of determining additional requirements from the system and options for improvement. Experiences gained from the preliminary study are taken into consideration in the development of the applications. The prototype to be developed must be further developed and evaluated in the long term. Subsequent studies should resolve any defects that might occur. The prototype is evaluated using the target group. Taking into account elderly people who suffer from dementia, it is also important to establish whether this system is accepted and can be used by dementia sufferers If it cannot be used, reasons need to be provided for this. In this, it must be established whether the system cannot be used due to the age of the sufferer or the illness. Although most older dementia sufferers today only have extremely limited knowledge of technology, it is not unreasonable to assume that early-stage dementia sufferers can in future be exposed to basic principles of dealing with technology in the earlier stages of the illness. As dementia sufferers have poor STM, it is almost impossible for them to recall at a later stage problems that occurred during use. Dementia patients are therefore

---

[4]In a semi-structured interview, the requested information is determined before the interview. The process, the sequence and the formulation of the questions are open, by contrast
[5]Glaser, B. (1977), p. 12

monitored while using technology, and are immediately questioned as to their opinion and suggestions for improvement.

2. State of research

This chapter is dedicated to current discussion in research areas of dementia and assistance systems for dementia sufferers. The nature and problems specific to dementia as an illness are presented. In this regard, the stages of dementia are explained, and the difficulties with which the sufferers are confronted at each stage listed. This is followed by an analysis of the use of different tools for persons suffering from dementia in the area of care, monitoring, support in everyday life and communication that have been researched up to now. In particular, the focus is on existing reminder and navigation systems for dementia sufferers.

2.1. Dementia

Advances in medicine and the rising standard of living contribute to an increase in life expectancy across the world. According to EUROSTAT, life expectancy in Europe in 2009 was 80.9 years[1] and is on an upward path. Researchers estimate that every second child born in Germany in 2007 could live to be 102 years old.[2]

The higher life expectancy also means an increase in the number of dementia sufferers. This in turn results in a reduction in life expectancy based on dementia. Although dementia is not a direct cause of death, it is often associated with complications that can lead to death.[3]

Life expectancy after diagnosis is 7 to 10 years.[4] The industrialised nations are currently more affected by the increase in dementia sufferers, where life expectancy is relatively high. As individuals age, so the chances that they will fall ill to dementia increase. At the age of 65, 3% of people are affected, but in 90-year-olds, the figure is 35%.[5] Consequently, the word

---

[1][Web/WKO]
[2][Web/DW]
[3][Web/AFI]
[4]Höwler, E. (2004) p. 2
[5]Weissenberger, M. (2009) p. 10

„dementia" is heard increasingly frequently in these countries. In Germany, over 1.2 million people suffer from dementia. Experts estimate that by 2030 the number of dementia sufferers in Germany will grow to 1.7 million.[6]

The word „dementia" is derived from the Latin, and means „away from the mind", „without the mind"or „without sense". Gerald Gatterer defines the concept of „dementia" as follows: „By dementia, according to international criteria, we understand a failure of memory and other cognitive functions such as speech, orientation, abstract thinking ability, motoric capacity, reading, numeracy and behaviour that are so serious that the affected person is noticeably hindered in most activities in everyday life.".[7] Dementia is not an illness, but rather a combination of different symptoms that can be caused by different brain diseases. One of the symptoms that is of central importance to this study is memory disturbance. A distinction is made between different forms of dementia. The primary form includes degenerative (Alzheimer's disease) and vascular forms, which have developed from brain damage. In the secondary forms, a distinction is made between irreversible (HIV, tumour) and reversible (vitamin B12 deficiency) forms that arise due to extra-cerebral damage. The most commonly occurring form is Alzheimer's disease, which was first described in 1907 by Alois Alzheimer. In this disease, the brain functions degenerate without external changes. Firstly, death of the nerve cells in the brain and their connections occurs. These are responsible for memory and information processing functions and are the locations where old information is combined with new, incoming information. The result is that sensible information processing is severely influenced. The progress of the disease is different from person to person. Symptoms are usually insidious, and are at first unnoticed, developing gradually. By the time a person suffers from massive forgetfulness, the brain has already been subjected to many years of severe changes. In younger people, the disease also progresses more rapidly than in older people.[8]

There is currently no cure for dementia, although its progress can be retarded by exercises and medication. Scientists are working on finding a means to stop the development of the illness as early as possible. The first successes have been recorded: Scientists in the Georgetown University Medical Center in Washington, D.C. have stopped Alzheimer's disease in mice using gene therapy.[9]

Table 2.1 shows the needs of individuals with an Alzheimer type, as well as possible mobile

---

[6]Gatterer, G. (2005) p. 11
[7]Gatterer, G. (2005) p. 10
[8]Gatterer, G. (2005) p. 17
[9][Web/Focus.de B]

support:

Symptoms / problems	Needs	Mobile phone applications
<ul><li>Memory problems</li><li>Problems in everyday life</li><li>Isolation</li><li>Disorientation</li><li>Lack of clear thought</li><li>Frustration</li><li>Misplacing objects</li><li>Mood swings</li></ul>	<ul><li>Memory</li><li>Directions</li><li>Socialisation</li><li>Notebook for medication</li><li>Relaxation</li><li>Activity monitoring and support</li></ul>	<ul><li>SMS/MMS</li><li>Multimedia messages</li><li>GPS</li><li>Internet chat/email/phone call</li><li>Video conference</li><li>Calendar</li><li>Listening to music</li></ul>

Table 2.1.: Symptoms, needs and possible mobile phone support for Alzheimer's sufferers[10]

The precise causes of the development of dementia are still unknown. Genetic factors and environmental influences are considered to be possible causes. Approximately 50 diseases have been listed as increasing the possibility of the development of dementia. The affected person is shocked at the onset of the illness, and denies the first symptoms, which means a timely diagnosis cannot be provided. From Table 2.2 it can be noted that the illness starts with small complaints and then develops over time, until the ability to speak is lost totally and the brain is practically morbid. The illness cannot be determined with certainty in the first two stages. In stages 3 and 4, the situation deteriorates noticeably; forgetfulness is prominent, the affected person forgets information that he has only recently acquired, he has immense difficulty with orientation in unfamiliar locations, and the temporal orientation is also disturbed. From stage 5, clear memory gaps are already present. The sufferer is dependent on external assistance. In the early stages, short-term memory is affected, and in the later stages long-term memory is increasingly vulnerable.[11]

---

[10]Armstrong, N. (2009)
[11]Gatterer, G. (2005) p. 10
[12]Gatterer, G. (2005) p. 18

Stage	Description	Duration	Lost abilities
1	Normal, no complaints	-	No problems
2	Subjective complaints	-	Light, subjective problems
3	Employees/relatives notice reduced work performance	7 years	Orientation at unfamiliar locations; working capacity
4	Reduced capacities for performing complex tasks (e.g. dinner, money matters, shopping)	2 years	Orientation at unfamiliar locations; simple financial activities
5	Independent existence without external aid not guaranteed	1,5 years	Selecting clothes
6	Loss of basic everyday capabilities	2,5 years	Dressing; washing
7	Loss of speech and motor skills	6 years and more	Speaking, walking, sitting, laughing

Table 2.2.: Stages of dementia[12]

The following symptoms of dementia are relevant to this study:

- Forgetting dates and current events that have only recently taken place
- Poor memory for names and faces
- Low decision-making capability
- Limited judgement capability
- Orientation difficulties in unfamiliar environments
- Difficulties when performing customary activities (work, household chores etc.)
- Temporal and spatial disorientation
- Loss of personal initiative
- (in the case of advanced dementia): confusion of the past and the present

A period of up to 10 years can elapse before a transition from stage 3 to 4 occurs, whereby the affected person is no longer able to live independently with certainty. Aspects of the relationship between caregivers and those cared for are of key importance. In the early stages of dementia, the sufferer is often cared for by relatives (husband/wife, son or daughter, son-in-law or daughter-in-law), friends or acquaintances of the sufferer. As is the case in any relationship, a great deal depends on the affected person as to what relationship an individual wishes to have with another person, the nature of his character and what anxieties, feelings of shame or anger exist, for example. Doctors, caregivers, patients or relatives are confronted with ethical issues. Ethical issues are often unclear for dementia sufferers, in the sense of what is morally right or wrong. The following ethical questions are most often raised by caregivers:

- To what extent should a manifestation of will be accepted?

- Should one allow the capabilities that were performed before dementia?

- How can the intent of the sufferer be fulfilled?

- What needs do dementia sufferers have, and how much latitude should they have?

These questions are difficult to answer, because one needs to know every dementia sufferer well, and all questions can only be answered individually for a sufferer. An afflicted person may often undertake something that he cannot, however, perform. A situation in which the affected person does not know how things will turn out can often be dangerous for him. This question also makes it more difficult for the caregiver to take a decision. But it is also extremely important that dementia sufferers do not have the feeling of being controlled permanently, which they perceive as an invasion of their privacy. Relatives cannot be seen as ideal substitutes as they do not know how to react in particular situations. Relatives cannot mask their painful feelings that are associated with the illness. In most cases people with dementia have the feeling of not being part of society, and of being an outsider and a pitied sufferer. This affects people more than the illness itself, which could lead to depression after diagnosis.

2.2. Concepts

The world is showing great interest in systems (for navigation, reminder, communication systems etc.) in different areas of life that make it easier for people to accomplish tasks and to reinforce their independence. The number and form of different systems that make our lives easier, increase self-confidence and promote independence grow daily. Besides the systems that are used in hospitals for diagnosis or treatment, the number of systems used for care and monitoring of illness sufferers or for supporting ill people or the elderly in their everyday activities is increasing. These new technologies can also be useful for dementia sufferers. The significance of dementia becomes clear when one examines the number of people suffering from dementia and the costs associated with this illness. In the future, the number of persons with dementia requiring care will rise even further. This however also means an increase in costs associated with care (personnel, doctors, homes etc.) In Germany alone, dementia is responsible for costs of over 9 billion Euro.[13] According to one study, the worldwide cost of treatment of dementia in 2010 was over 604 billion.[14] From a social and economic perspective, it is extremely important that dementia sufferers are able to perform tasks themselves, without external assistance, for a long period of time. This provides relief to formal and informal caregivers, and improves the living conditions of the sufferer.

A number of associations and companies exist in the EU (European Alzheimer - Societies 2009) that provide support for people with dementia and their caregivers. These are often informative websites that provide useful information for caregivers. However, the information on these websites is usually not geared towards the dementia sufferer. New technologies can however compensate for deficits in memory, orientation and communication. Various studies have shown[15], that people with mild to moderate dementia can benefit from these technologies. These tools are however mostly aimed at users who are already well versed in modern technology. Most elderly people, in particular dementia sufferers, are almost completely isolated from these technologies, though. Yet despite all these new initiatives, additional support for care personnel is required. In this regard, the aim is to improve the quality of life of dementia sufferers and to provide relief to caregivers. For this reason, differences in opinion between dementia sufferers and caregivers must be taken note of. Assessments of caregivers and families in terms of the needs of dementia sufferers differ from the opinion

---

[13][Web/DEStatis.de]
[14][Web/AZK]
[15]Liu, R. (2009); Kaminoyama, H. (2007); Goodman, J. (2004) (C), (2005) (D); Hagethorn, F. N. (2008); Hile, H. (2008); Veldkamp, D. (2008); etc.

of the sufferers. Various studies have shown that the opinions of caregivers depend on the individual psychological condition of the caregiver.[16] Dröes lists 7 key areas[17] that can be used to assess the quality of life of dementia sufferers:

- Physical and psychological health
- Social contacts with family and friends
- Benefits for others
- Performing daily activities
- Feeling of self-worth
- Self-determination
- Freedom

Many technologies are already available for dementia sufferers. These technologies are designed to remind dementia sufferers of everyday activities, to support them and to help them to maintain social contacts and avoid dangerous situations. The studies have shown that dementia sufferers themselves refer to information (in terms of treatment, care and support, and arrangements), communication, meaningful daily activities and physical failures.[18] The different technical solutions can be divided into four areas as a result of the COGKNOW[19] research project:[20]

- Reminder support
- Technologies for supporting everyday activities
- Support for social contacts (communication and interaction)
- Safety support and monitoring

Es ist wichtig zu verstehen, dass es keine alleinige Lösung für demente Menschen gibt, die alle Bereiche laut COGKNOW abdeckt.

It is important to understand that there is no single solution for people with dementia that covers all areas according to COGKNOW. In terms of reminder support, various devices have

---

[16]Hancock, G. A. (2003)
[17]Dröes, R. M. (2006)
[18]Mailand, F. J. M. (2007)
[19]COGKNOW is a pan-European research project that has investigated options for support of early-stage dementia sufferers since 2006
[20]Mailand, F. J. M. (2007)

15

been developed for cognitive reinforcement and reminder support in the EU project Technology, Ethics and Dementia (TED) as part of the EU programme Biomedicine and Health. An example of this is the Forget-Me-Not device, an electronic calendar that supports people suffering from memory problems. Researchers have established that this device can be used by people who are limited by temporal orientation problems. ENABLE (Enabling Technologies for People with Dementia) is an example of technology for support in everyday activities. These examine the effect of the assistance device in supporting memory, happiness and convenience, improving communication for people with dementia with reference to their quality of life and the load on caregiving personnel. An analysis of the needs examined in various studies shows the importance of different areas of life. This includes not only the feeling of independence, support in temporal and spatial disorientation and memory problems, but also communication. In this area, a mobile phone has been developed with a call button for elderly people with cognitive disabilities. This phone enables rapid contact with family or caregivers (MOBILE Tele-Coach, MORE-phone[21]). Various studies have confirmed positive social experiences and a positive effect on self-confidence in some dementia sufferers in relation to mobile phones with a call button. Some users were not satisfied with the design of the special mobile phone.[22] Facilitating communication achieves not only a reinforcement of identity and memory in the dementia sufferer but also motivates the affected person to express his own opinions, thoughts, wishes and fears, leading to a strengthening of the feeling that he is part of society. The fourth area is that of safety support and monitoring. This area is concerned with devices designed to prevent dementia sufferers from being exposed to dangerous situations. The number of scientific studies that investigate the results of these devices for dementia sufferers is however small. Miskelly has investigated the use of an electronic identification system for dementia sufferers in homes. The result of this study shows that this type of system is safe and can be successfully used for determining when patients move around. The system can also be used by homes that accommodate persons other than dementia sufferers.[23]

A focus area for the development of systems for support in everyday activities is on systems that alleviate difficulties faced by older dementia sufferers within their house. An example of this is the system for monitoring administration of medication of dementia patients as described in the study by Fook and Tee[24]. It is critical for doctors to know whether dementia patients are taking their daily medicines to be able to prescribe the correct dosage and to be

---

[21] Mobile phones that have been specially developed for communication by dementia sufferers
[22] Mulvenna, M. (2010)
[23] Miskelly, F. (2004)
[24] Fook, V. F. S. (2007)

able to give correct advice on care. This information is normally collected by the caregivers or even by the patients themselves. Incorrect information can result in the wrong treatment being prescribed, which could lead to catastrophic consequences. The new system is based on a wireless, multimodal sensor, an actor and a mobile phone, and reminds the patient about taking medicines, as well as providing information that can be called up on a mobile phone at any time for doctors and care personnel. Besides a good recognition rate and the minimisation of false alarms, the system is designed not to change the patient's life and not to be intrusive. The problems related to monitoring in terms of design, implementation and provision of the system are also discussed. In addition, the behaviour of the patient and the provision of speech, image and text prompts andreminders are examined to be able to support patients in medication-based treatment. Other, similar systems that support dementia sufferers during treatment at home have been described by Wherton and Monk[25] and Biswas and Mokhtari[26]. These indoor systems are aimed at monitoring the activities of dementia sufferers or elderly persons not suffering from dementia, and send information to the caregiver in an emergency.

New technologies such as GPS allow tracking and support in various situations. The use of a tracking device such as this can contribute to improved safety of older persons or dementia sufferers, as they can quickly become lost due to their defective sense of orientation, which represents a high degree of risk for the person concerned. Relatives providing care are extremely concerned and wish to ensure that everything is being done to protect the affected persons. Chip implants are also used for this purpose. The decision to use these systems is however a complex ethical question[27] that must be weighed up against autonomy and privacy. For this reason, outdoor systems are also being developed for dementia sufferers and older people, in addition to indoor systems. The tendency to run away that often appears in dementia patients is an important reason for using a system such as this for monitoring and location of sufferers in the advanced stages of the illness.

Alzheimer monitoring is a research project performed by the University of Siegen and ITSS solutions+ systems GmbH. The aim of this study is to examine whether a location system could be used for dementia patients. Sufferers would then wear a GPS device that would send their location to a server via a wireless link. This data can then be called up on the internet at any time by caregivers. Systems such as these are already used today in old-age homes and hospitals where dementia patients are treated. One problem in the use of these systems is that dementia sufferers often refuse to wear these GPS devices (or forget

---

[25]Wherton, J. P. (2008)

[26]Biswas, J. (2010)

[27]Additional information on who makes the decision as to use can be found in the study by Landaua, R. (2010)

to take the device with them). A useful solution would be to use GPS devices in the form of wrist watches or shoes. Use in this form however raises ethical questions again as it could intrude upon the privacy of the patient. The study by Dale shows that this solution can be used successfully for locating dementia sufferers when they cannot be traced. [28]

An additional study on locating dementia patients was performed by Fudickar and Schnor at the University of Potsdam.[30] Besides monitoring, the system developed enables communication between patients and caregivers, and reminders and administration of appointments. A voice-based user interface was suggested for operating the tool. The study showed that dementia patients hardly use mobile phones at all (see Figure 2.2). Seven dementia sufferers and 10 caregivers were interviewed.[31]

Figure 2.1.: GPS wrist watch[29]

GPS tracking systems are mainly used in the advanced stages of dementia, although they can be used in the early stages. In these early stages, the affected person can still perform some functions himself. To this end, the patients require systems that assist them with these tasks. In the early stages of dementia, navigation and reminder systems can be implemented that would be of no use in patients in the advanced stages.

The research field for dementia patients in the early stages is discussed in greater detail below. As already mentioned, dementia starts with a memory problem and progresses until the patient loses speech and motor control. Reminder tools can be a useful solution for patients in the early stages of dementia. By means of cognitive support, the user's feeling of being independent can be reinforced and his quality of life improved. Reminder tools are normally time-based, event-based, location-specific or hybrid and context-related[33], as a mixture of the first three forms. In the case of context-related reminder tools, rules are used to decide whether an event

[28]Dale, Ø. (2008)
[29]Lou, R. C. (2010)
[30]Fudickar, S. (2009)
[31]Fudickar, S. (2011)
[32]Own figure (based on data from Fudickar, S. (2011))
[33]Du, K. (2008)

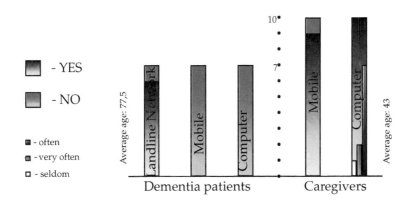

Figure 2.2.: Use of mobile phones and computers in dementia patients and caregivers[32]

should be triggered. The rules can be added or modified by the caregiver using special tools. Until recently, all strategies and measures were based on assessments by the caregiver or the family of the dementia patient, and not on the patient's views and his own needs. There are only a few studies in which the opinion of dementia sufferers as to their own needs is described. This is also related to the fact that dementia patients are extremely reluctant to discuss dementia and difficulties associated with the illness; for many people, dementia is a taboo topic. Another issue is that dementia sufferers are often not taken seriously and very little attention is paid to their opinion. Various studies have shown that navigation systems used for elderly people can be useful if they are developed using some consideration.[34]

For people who have difficulties finding their way in internal and external areas, both simple and complex navigation systems have been developed. The tool[35] consists of two parts that the person wears, one on the left side and one on the right side. A vibration on either side indicates the required direction of travel for the wearer. Studies for relatively complex, landmark-based navigation systems have been undertaken by Liu and Hile, Kaminoyama and Matsuo, Goodman and Brewster, Hagethorn and Kröse, and Hile Vedantham[36]. The subject carries a mobile phone with GPS and internet access. Depending on where the person is located (GPS coordinates), images of nearby objects are loaded onto the mobile phone via

---

[34]Goodman, J. (2004) (A)
[35]Grierson, L. E. M. (2011)
[36]Liu, R. (2009); Kaminoyama, H. (2007); Goodman, J. (2004) (C), (2005) (D); Hagethorn, F. N. (2008); Hile, H. (2008)

the internet. The downloaded image is extended by means of a direction arrow and text (additionally, audio messages are downloaded for each orientation point), making orientation easier for the person. Results of these studies show that landmark-based navigation systems can be used successfully. Their success rate is higher than that for map-based navigation systems. However, the directions for landmark-based navigation systems must be carefully formulated.[37] Goodman reports a higher degree of success using a landmark-based system for elderly people than for younger people. However, images for similar orientation points can confuse people.

Finding one's way using a navigation system can also be dangerous for dementia patients in the early stages of the illness. Hagethorn and Kröse[39] have addressed this question, observing that dangerous walking behaviour occurred during pedestrian navigation when crossing a street (the affected persons crossed the street without looking out for vehicular traffic). By contrast, Hetting and De Boer[40] found no signs of dangerous walking behaviour when using mobile navigation.

Figure 2.3.: Landmark-based navigation[38]

This study was however performed on a small group of dementia patients, and dangerous walking behaviour can consequently not be ruled out.

In the study by Hagethorn, patients and caregivers were asked about their opinions on functions that were essential for pedestrian navigation:

- Based on reduced perceptual ability of the dementia patient, the navigation tool should only have a few buttons.

- Due to decreased motor skills, the buttons should be large.

---

[37]Veldkamp, D. (2008); Hagethorn, F. N. (2008)
[38]Hile, H. (2008)
[39]Hagethorn, F. N. (2008)
[40]Hetting, M. (2009)

- The navigation tool should be as easy to operate as possible, so that the patient can navigate himself.

- It would be desirable if the navigation tool supported „leisurely strolling". This is defined as the option to deviate from a route, but to then be able to navigate to the starting point again if the navigator has strayed too far.

- The tool should contain a calling button to facilitate communication with the caregiver in case help is required.

- The tool should have a tracking function so that caregivers can locate the patients.

The significance of tool design for dementia sufferers was investigated by Marquardt.[41] The results of this study were the hypotheses identified from considered design studies for supporting the spatial orientation of people with dementia and to help them find their way. According to Marquardt, the following key aspects should be considered when developing dementia-friendly support tools:

- The tool should be usable without the user having to acquire new, complicated skills. The learning capabilities of dementia sufferers are limited; consequently, operation of the tool should not require reading and interpretation of material.

- The tool should enable visual access and retain an overview. Dementia sufferers cannot represent spatial locations.

- Decision making should be reduced to a minimum. Making the correct decision is difficult for dementia patients and is associated with additional stress.

- The architectural readability should be high. The sizes and shapes should be similar to real life. This enables dementia patients to remember information more easily.

Although all four areas cover different needs for an independent life for dementia sufferers, they are almost always associated with the reminder function. As a result, support tools are usually equipped with a reminder function. Examples of pure reminder systems are the systems described by Du and Zhang[42] and by Carmichael and Rice[43].

Almost all tools for dementia patients contain notification systems, be they reminder systems or navigation systems. Notifications in tools are normally acoustic. In this regard, Winkler

---

[41]Marquardt, G. (2011)
[42]Du, K. (2008)
[43]Carmichael, A. (2008)

and Cowan[44] conducted a study on speech recognition in people. The results of this study indicate that acoustic information is retained better by individuals, is processed more quickly, and can be stored in the memory for a relatively long time. If an acoustic notification is perceived again, people automatically tend to react to the notification. As can be seen, the spectrum of support tools is extremely wide. Various tools have been developed for dementia sufferers that provide support in everyday life, including navigation and memory assistance. Numerous studies report the success of landmark-based navigation systems, the importance of memory support and support by means of communication with the caregiver. In my study, I will attempt to combine all these functions into one navigation tool for pedestrians, and to examine the usefulness of this tool by means of evaluation after implementation. In addition, the advantages and disadvantages of using AR for pedestrian navigation for dementia patients will be researched. The following chapter deals with the preliminary study and its results. Knowledge gained from interviews with dementia patients and caregivers as well as from events on the topic of dementia will be presented.

---

[44]Winkler, I. (2005)

3. Preliminary study

The preliminary study provides the necessary knowledge for the actual study. This knowledge is derived from interviews and observation logs of dementia sufferers and their relatives or caregivers. A good knowledge of the field of study is required for the preliminary study, and the quality of the results depends on the preliminary study. Previous knowledge in hypotheses is confirmed or contradicted in the preliminary study by comparing the previous knowledge with hypotheses from the preliminary study. New hypotheses from interviews and observations are created, as the area to be researched is still relatively unexplored and little literature can be found. They are intended to contribute to covering the needs of potential users as well as possible. Hypotheses should be formulated for both user technical questions as well as for illness and age-specific factors. The following sub-chapter describes the methods used for gathering information and content analysis of the interviews. The results of the preliminary study are then summarised.

3.1. Methodology

The target group of persons to be interviewed consists of people with poor STM (mainly dementia patients who are at least in the psychological position of being able to answer questions) and their relatives and/or caregivers. In various studies, researchers refer to the fact that the dementia patients themselves are not spoken to in many studies, rather they are spoken about. However, without taking into account the thoughts of the affected persons, problems associated with the illness cannot be completely understood. To close this gap and to include users of the system to be developed in the development process, interviews will be conducted with the dementia patients before development. The opinion of the caregivers should not however be ignored, due to the physical and psychological condition of the dementia sufferers. Consequently, the dementia patients' caregivers will also be questioned. I decided on the open, partially standardised guideline interview for gathering information. The questions are pre-formulated, but the manner of answering is at the discretion of the interviewee. It is possible to deviate from the interview guidelines. It became evident at a later stage that partially standardised interviews with dementia patients were not always possible, as they sometimes did not accept that they were ill. Some interviews were then conducted as free-form discussions, whereby the interviewee was encouraged to discuss issues freely, which naturally made gathering and evaluation of information difficult.[1] Where questions were not answered or were answered incompletely, the interviewee was prodded for further explanation. As dementia patients are extremely reluctant to speak about their illness, non-thematic questions play an essential role in hypothesis generation, which must also be subjectively interpreted, however. Description of the problems and their solutions is reserved for the interviewees to ensure that their actual opinion on central questions is heard. Due to the openness of the interviews, the discussions were recorded for improved evaluation where permission to do so was granted. However, where discussions are recorded people can feel ill at ease. Consequently, a confidential and pleasant discussion atmosphere must be created by means of a gentle interview technique.[2] A pleasant, confidential atmosphere for dementia patients is particularly important, due to their psychological state and the social and mental pressure under which they and their relatives constantly find themselves. In this manner, it was possible to gather as much information as possible from the interviewees.

The empirical data (interview transcripts and logs, observation logs, documents etc.) serves as the source of the information to be evaluated. Interview transcripts were prepared from the sound recording of the interviews. This was followed by a content analysis, which was designed to reduce the text to its significant components in such a manner that the core statements were distilled. Inductive category formation is an important technique used here.[3] Hypotheses and theories were generated from this empirical data. The evaluation strategy was performed cyclically, that is, the research steps were executed numerous times. This enabled insights from different evaluations to be linked together and the hypothesis and theory generation to be progressed. Evaluation during the data gathering process influenced the following discussions. To prepare for the summary, the coding and context units were defined. A coding unit is the smallest text component that can be allocated to one of the categories created. Every statement made by the interviewee on a relevant issue was considered to be a coding unit, and all answers in a questionnaire were considered a context unit.

---

[1] The topic of acceptance is discussed further in the following sub-chapter
[2] Gentle interview technique means creating a mutual trust relationship with the interviewee, to show personal sympathy
[3] Mayring, P. (2010)

Evaluation was performed in four steps, according to Mayring (rules[4] for summary content analysis).[5]

Hypotheses were formed from the evaluation. In general, statements can be deemed to be hypotheses if they meet these three requirements:[6]

- The statements must in principle be able to fail according to experiences (criterion of provability), that is, they must be contradictable.

- The statements must be related to one another in a recognisable manner, and must refer to the same subject matter.

- The statements must be logically compatible with one another (criterion of internal consistency).

A description of the results follows the hypothesis generation. The results are used later in the following chapter together with the insights from the research fields as a basis for identification of requirements. The next sub-chapter describes the questions and problems arising from the preliminary study.

---

[4]Appendix F
[5]Mayring, P. (2010)
[6]Kromrey, K. (2002) p. 54

3.2. Results

A study of persons in the early stages of dementia is not easy. Besides the problem of even finding early-stage dementia patients to interview, questioning interviewees was not unproblematic for both the patients and for the caregivers due to the psychological complexity of the topic. Three out of four interviewees did not consider themselves to be patients, and felt that they were healthy. Dementia was seen as a „long goodbye", as death. Persons with dementia were viewed as requiring sympathy, which places an additional burden on the patients. It could be a number of years before people accept that they are suffering from dementia. This is also a difficult topic for caregivers, as they are responsible for the affected person and are concerned about them. In the early stages, the caregivers are often relatives. All these aspects influence the course of the interviews and the answers supplied. In many cases this resulted in false answers being given, which complicated the interview and the analysis. A central topic in dementia, at least in the early stages, is the patients' feeling of shame. This feeling influences or even determines the answers, which was however also the case for communication with the caregiver. In many cases, the feeling of shame led to secrecy about the illness, which can result in the patient declining assistance. The search for dementia patients was also not uncomplicated. Firstly, because the tool to be developed is intended for early-stage dementia sufferers, it was problematic finding people with early-stage dementia who were psychologically and physically capable of fulfilling various tasks themselves. In many cases, people with early-stage dementia hide the illness from the rest of society. Secondly, they often did not wish to participate in interviews because the caregivers doubted that the navigation tool could be operated by dementia patients. In addition, the caregivers feared that the interviews and the tool could cause additional stress. The analysis from Table 3.1 answers the questions and confirms a number of problems of people with dementia and their caregivers.

Table 3.1.: Evaluation of interviews

No	InVw	InPa	Time	Paraphrasing	Generalisation	Reduction
1	B	BI	00:25:21	She is permanently looking for things	Memory problems in dementia	Dementia:
2	C	BI	00:11:21	She cannot find her things; forgets birthday		① Proceeds insidiously
						② Body follows dementia
3	D	BI	00:45:25	She sorts objects again, permanently looking for things		③ Same sequence important
						④ Strangers' impressions can be deceptive
4	A	DI	00:03:45	Enters the wrong train	Spatial disorientation in dementia	
5	A	DI	00:03:45	Don't know where I am		Dementia patients:
6	A	BI	00:21:20	Last time you were wrong when you told me where you were		① Set high expectations and
7	A	DI	00:03:45	My dog must help me first; if not, I will call my wife	In emergencies, dementia patients cannot cope on their own	② Become angry/aggressive if they don't manage something
8	A	DI	00:05:45	(In an emergency) We make a lot of phone calls	Location/help by conventional means (telephonic)	③ Try to shift their own shortcomings onto others
9	A	DI	00:05:17	My wife helps me	In early stages, relatives cope without professional support	④ It's not good to leave familiar environments
10	A	BI	00:05:55	It's a strain to work yourself. I need something to relieve the burden	Supporting dementia patients is stressful, burdensome	Acceptance problem in dementia patients due to:
11	B	BI	00:07:46	My health and nerves are suffering		① Feeling of shame
12	C	BI	00:07:17	Sometimes I just need quiet		② Knowledge that they can't do some things any more
13	A	BI	00:07:45	He's going to work	People with mild dementia can hold a job	③ Loss of autonomy
14	A	BI	00:14:30	He's having ergotherapy and physiotherapy	Visit different locations alone	④ Internal power Struggles:
15	A	DI	00:08:12	I always have problems orienting myself	Spatial disorientation in dementia patients	• Character intensification • Personal conflicts become active

No	InVv	InPa	Time	Paraphrasing	Generalisation	Reduction
16	A	DI	00:08:12	If I go somewhere foreign, I have great difficulties	No (or very poor) spatial orientation at foreign locations	Early-stage dementia patients suffer from:
17	C	BI	00:17:36	She cannot orient herself at foreign locations		① Memory problems:
18	D	BI	00:09:00	No orientation at foreign locations		▪ Relatively good LTM
19	D	DI	00:04:08	Dementia patients definitely can't go walking alone		▪ Very poor STM
20	A	DI	00:08:12	I find the way if I have driven this way many times before	Relatively good spatial orientation at known locations	− Very difficult to learn something new
21	B	BI	00:10:31	She never walks alone, she would always find the way home, though		
22	C	BI	00:17:36	She goes shopping alone, but she always finds the way home		② Temporal disorientation
23	C	DI	00:30:37	I like going walking alone		③ Spatial temporal disorientation:
24	D	BI	00:56:39	Here in the village, she would always be able to find her way home		▪ Light disorient. at known locations
25	B	BI	00:10:31	Here in the village everyone knows her	Residential area should be considered when formulating needs for navigation assistance	▪ Complete disorient. at foreign locations
26	C	BI	00:17:36	Here in the village everyone knows her		
27	A	BI	00:08:30	This is a problem of both the route and time	Temporal disorientation in dementia patients	Dementia for caregivers:
28	A	BI	00:08:30	Important to be at the right place at the right time (greatest difficulty)	Temporal and spatial support required for dementia	① Is stressful, burdensome
29	A	BI	00:09:45	Tool should provide acoustic reminder for events	Acoustic reminders are better perceived	② Is more of a psychological than a physical burden
30	A	BI	00:39:20	Notes are no good at all; must be an acoustic signal		③ Means learning continuously
31	D	BI	00:24:03	Acoustic is good		④ It is difficult to keep calm

---

No	InVw	InPa	Time	Paraphrasing	Generalisation	Reduction
32	A	DI	00:10:00	I can't use a mobile phone with touchscreen	Deficits in hand motor skills in dementia	A special assistance tool for dementia patients is important because:
33	A	BI	00:10:40	He has his old mobile phone again		
34	A	BI	00:14:30	The tool should be for patients	It should be as easy as possible to use the tool	① They show temporal and spatial disorientation, besides memory problems
35	A	DI	00:16:45	It is important that the tool reminds me to press the button	Dementia patients can forget how they can be helped	② They are helpless if alone in an emergency
36	A	BI	00:14:30	... with a large red button and it must glow in the dark		③ People with mild dementia can hold a job
37	D	BI	00:24:03	A green button so that I can see it		④ It is important to be able to perform some tasks oneself
38	A	DI	00:16:45	I will use it if it really helps me	The tool should contain a number of functions for help	⑤ Will not place extra load on the caregiver
39	A	BI	00:36:37	In dementia, it's important to always have the same sequence	In dementia, it's important to always have the same sequence	Advantages for the caregiver of an assistance tool:
40	A	DI BI	00:37:00	Everything I could do before dementia I can still do; it's new things that I can't do, though	Poor STM in mild dementia, relatively good LTM	① Assistance using conventional methods is very difficult in an emergency
41	D	BI	01:26:15	Everything she could do before dementia she can still do; it's new things that she can't do, though		② In the early stages, caregivers are relatives who do not have professional knowledge about support, which could mean frequent emergencies
42	B	BI	00:03:18	People who don't know the patient think that this person is totally	First impression by strangers can be deceptive	③ Support is burdensome, stressful
43	B	BI	00:03:18	Sometimes one reacts too strongly	It's sometimes difficult for caregivers to stay	④ Caregivers want to know when their help is required
44	B	BI	00:03:18	Mother-daughter conflict	Personal conflicts become active	⑤ Additional safety offered

No	InV	InPa	Time	Paraphrasing	Generalisation	Reduction
45	B	BI	00:03:18	Difficult to accept that she is reliant on my help	Autonomy	Following reasons mentioned for not using special assistance tools for dementia patients:
46	B	BI	00:03:18	Difficult to accept that she can no longer do certain things (because of shame)	No acceptance of illness (due to feeling of shame)	
47	C	BI	00:11:21	If she forgets to do something, she tries to explain it by saying she will do it straight away		① At a location (e.g. in a village) that the dementia patient knows from his LTM, and in which he goes walking in the area, and
48	B	BI	00:03:18	She blames others for her own deficits	Dementia patients try to blame others for their deficits	
49	C	BI	00:03:35	She says that she's not forgetful, rather we are		② If everyone knows him at this location, the dementia patient can manage without an assistance tool
50	D	BI	00:06:32	She tries to blame others for her own deficits		
51	B	BI	00:06:34	Dementia always follows the body	Motor skills deficits increase with dementia	
52	B	BI	00:07:46	Change happens very insidiously	Dementia progresses insidiously	③ Deficits in (hand) motor skills
53	B	BI	00:07:46	Changing location brings a number of stumbling blocks	Changing location has a negative effect on dementia patients due to poor STM and relatively good LTM	④ Domestic caregivers believe that the dementia patient cannot operate a new device
54	B	BI	00:10:31	She starts something, can't manage and becomes angry	Dementia patients set high standards and become angry if they cannot manage something and their deficits are detected	⑤ Monitoring binds the caregiver to the person again
55	C	BI	00:03:35	She can't do much however and some-times becomes angry as a result		
56	B	BI	00:06:34	She becomes aggressive because she's unhappy	Dementia patients can become aggressive	
57	B	BI	00:21:25	She can't handle computers or mobile phones	No technical knowledge due to age and poor STM	

No	InVi	InPa	Time	Paraphrasing	Generalisation	Reduction
58	B	BI	00:21:25	She would be overwhelmed by such a tool	Caregivers think dementia patients can't operate tools like this	Opinion of dementia patients and caregivers as to requirements of an assistance tool:
59	D	BI	00:48:53	She can't handle the remote control (due to illness) (maybe for younger generation)		① The tool should contain temporal **and** spatial support
60	B	BI	00:35:41	She doesn't want to lose her autonomy	Autonomy is particularly important for dementia patients	② Notifications should be acoustic
61	B	BI	00:36:51	Huge difficulty: acceptance of being reliant on others		③ Deficits in motor skills should be considered
62	B	BI	00:36:51	She doesn't want to be a burden on me	Unpleasant being a burden on others	④ The tool should be easy to operate
63	C	DI	00:32:03	I don't want to be a burden on my daughter		⑤ The tool should match requirements
64	B	BI	00:53:36	(Monitoring) a system like this creates a tight link again	Monitoring binds you to the person to be monitored	⑥ The tool should remind dementia patients about possible help functions
65	B	BI	00:57:00	In dementia, it's not physical work, but rather what's in your head that doesn't leave you alone	Psychological load for the caregiver	⑦ The tool should be based on existing technical knowledge (due to age and illness)
66	C	BI	00:11:21	She was a domineering woman	Character is intensified in dementia	
67	D	BI	00:00:35	She is bossy		
68	C	BI	00:18:45	I need something that makes me aware that she needs me now	Monitoring and notification in an emergency	⑧ The caregiver should know when help is needed
69	C	DI	00:41:54	I don't mind others helping me	External help is accepted	⑨ The tool should not be called an „assistance tool" (due to acceptance problems)
70	C	DI	00:43:17	I understand that in old age you can no longer do various things	People understand that they can't do everything themselves any more	
71	C	DI	00:53:10	(Monitoring) I'm not against it	Monitoring doesn't mean a loss of privacy for everyone	⑩ Complex system would overwhelm dementia patients
72	D	BI	01:03:20	(Monitoring) In this state it's not an invasion of privacy		
73	D	BI	01:23:40	Yes, the tool should not be called an „assistance tool"		

31

No	InVw	InPa	Time	Paraphrasing	Generalisation	Reduction
74	D	BI	00:29:34	I want to walk alone sometimes	Important to be able to perform some tasks alone	

InVw - Interview	InPa - Interviewee	DI - Dementia patient	BI - Caregiver

It is only when one delves deep into the topic of dementia that one realises how complex the subject is. Dealing with dementia patients requires an understanding that an interdependency exists in terms of the relationship between dementia patients and caregivers, the depression that they suffer from, the attitude of society to dementia, the physical and psychological state of the dementia patients and the physical and psychological state of relatives who are deeply concerned about the patients.

A total of three interviews were conducted with early-stage dementia patients and four interviews with their domestic caregivers. When interviewing dementia patients, it is important to distinguish between those who accept being ill with dementia and who accept that memory problems and other problems are a result of the illness, and those who reject

Age	Gender	Diagnosed since
Dementia patients		
47	Male	Brain atrophy 2010
86	Female	2007
92	Female	2009
87	Female	2010
Caregiver		
-	Female	-
48	Female	-
70	Female	-
-	Female	-

Table 3.2.: Interviewees

the thought of dementia. The answering behaviour in the interview is dependent on this. As opposed to patients in the first category who may be open about their problems, allowing actual requirements to be established, it is necessary to take into account that the patients in the second category attempt to hide their actual requirements.

Table 3.1 shows the results of the analysis. The results confirm many aspects of existing knowledge in these areas of research. Dementia progresses insidiously, and dementia patients suffer from memory problems, and temporal and spatial disorientation, whereby orientation at known locations is better than at unfamiliar locations. Dementia patients are unable to orient themselves at foreign locations and cannot cope without external assistance. The interview analysis shows that the use of the navigation system for people with dementia in the early stages could be extremely helpful. The system can provide safety for the dementia sufferer as

32

well as for the caregiver. It is extremely important for the caregiver to know when the person cared for needs help. In addition, the system can relieve the caregiver of a burden and assist the dementia patient in becoming self-reliant. Relieving the load for the caregiver has both economic and personal benefits to the caregiver. This load can lead to the patient not being well cared for. Autonomy is important for every individual, but it is particularly important for dementia patients, as they are reliant on external assistance in many cases, giving them the feeling that they are not free. Richard Taylor, who suffers from Alzheimer's disease says in his book „Alzheimer's from the inside out"that he „is ashamed"to ask his wife for assistance when he does not know where he is and what he should do.[7] From the statement and from interviews it becomes clear that everyday activities can be performed independently by dementia patients, and that they require something that can assist them in the process. Another very important insight is that a navigation system without a reminder function is of no use in this stage of dementia. The reminder function can be seen as one of the most important requirements in dementia. Two out of three dementia patients stated that they found it good that relatives or caregivers looked after them and they had nothing against the caregiver knowing where they were. All four interviewees were of the opinion that people in this condition should be monitored. The next chapter lists the requirements of the system and the technologies required for realisation of the requirements.

---

[7] Taylor, R. (2008) p. 122

4. Conception

In this chapter, reasons are provided for the selection of technology, and technologies used for the realisation of requirements of the tools to be developed are described. These requirements affect both the function and the design of the tool. In this regard, mobile devices are compared with one another to be able to implement the tool for the most suitable device.

4.1. Requirements

The requirements are based on knowledge obtained from the research fields and the preliminary study. Requirements of usability and user interfaces are based on ISO norm EN ISO 9241 (11 & 110). It is particularly important that the requirements are observed due to the age and the psychological and physical state of the users. Requirements based on ISO 9241 are not discussed in more detail.

The system should consist of two subsystems; one for dementia patients that is designed to assist them in orientation, and the other for caregivers that is designed to enable administration and monitoring, that is, remote support. In this regard, the information necessary for supporting orientation should be made available to the caregiver. The following sub-chapter provides an overview of the requirements of a navigation tool. This is followed by a description of the requirements of the administration/monitoring tool.

4.1.1. Requirements of the navigation tool

As already mentioned in the preliminary study, a special device would not be a suitable solution for dementia sufferers, particularly because of the feeling of shame experienced by many patients. Consequently, the system should be developed for mobile phones. Results in the research fields have demonstrated the successful implementation of landmark-based navigation tools for dementia patients in contrast to map-based navigation. For this reason, the navigation tool to be developed should include navigation based on Augmented Reality. An additional important aspect derived from the research fields and the preliminary study is the knowledge that navigation for dementia patients is of no use without a reminder function. For this reason, the tool should contain navigation, location and communication functions as well as reminder functions.

Besides the requirements of ISO norm EN ISO 9241-11(110), the navigation tool will be based on the dementia-specific requirements described in the studies by Hagerthorn and by Marquardt.[1] Based on these requirements, and on the results of the empirical preliminary study, the following requirements of the system to be developed were derived:

- The potential users of the assistance tool are normally old people who are not familiar with modern technology

- Dementia means poor STM, whereby it is almost impossible to learn something new

- The tool will include both visual and acoustic notifications

- Decision-making should be kept to a minimum

- Support should be close to reality

- The tool should contain a Help button that enables communication with caregivers

    - In total, only one large, green button so that the user is not overwhelmed in an emergency

    - This button should be designated the „call button" due to the feeling of shame

- The call button should be large due to the (hand) motor skills deficit

- The tool will be remotely controlled and configured by caregivers

- Using the help button enables communication with the caregiver and location

- The tool will provide an acoustic reminder to dementia patients that they should use the help button in an emergency

Table 4.1 shows the requirements of the navigation tool:

---

[1]Chapter 2.2

No	Function	Description	Support
1	Navigation	The tool should assist dementia patients in going from one location to another	(++)
2	Acoustic assistance in navigation	Dementia patients receive acoustic notifications that assist in finding the way	(+)
3	Location	Caregiver should be able to locate the dementia patient	(++)
4	Monitoring only in an emergency	The tool can be set up in such a manner that the caregiver can only locate the dementia patient in an emergency	(+)
5	Permanent monitoring	The tool can be set up in such a manner that the caregiver can permanently monitor the dementia patient	(+)
6	Communication	Dementia patients should be able to communicate with the caregiver in an emergency	(++)
7	Recognition of an emergency	The tool should detect of its own accord whether the dementia patient needs help, based on prede-fined conditions	(++)
8	Acoustic notification in an emergency	Dementia patients receive an acoustic notification as to how they should do what (press call button)	(+)
9	Automatic help call	The tool can be set up in such a manner that it automatically connects to the caregiver in an emergency	(+)
10	Active support	Dementia patients should be able to phone the caregiver at any time	(+)
11	Reminder function	The tool reminds the dementia patient if there is a new route	(++)
12	Passive mode	For reasons of mobility, the tool should use as little battery power as possible	(+)
13	Changing the route	The route cannot be changed by the dementia patient, only by the caregiver	(-)

Table 4.1.: Requirements of the navigation tool

The navigation tool should detect an emergency, whereby the distance of the user from the route is calculated. If the user is more than 36 metres from the route or a point en route has not been reached at a predefined point in time, the tool should categorise the situation as an emergency. To assist in support by the caregiver, the situation of the dementia patient should be reflected for the caregiver as close to reality as possible. In this regard, data such as GPS position, heading and video data should be transmitted, in addition to an audio stream. The following sub-chapter describes the requirements of the administration/monitoring tool.

From discussions with dementia patients and caregivers, and from research fields, it has become clear that dementia patients are often unwilling to carry a special device, even when this could help them. This is linked to the fact that they are ashamed of their illness. Consequently, it would be sensible not to use a special device for this purpose, but rather to use a mobile phone. In addition, the navigation tool should not be called an assistance tool due to the feeling of shame, and the application should not refer to the fact that the user suffers from dementia.

The hardware requirements of the device to be developed as a navigation tool are as follows:

- High-performance processor for real-time calculations such as AR calculations and navigation function

- Mobile internet for data, audio and video data transmission (it is important to use 3G technology due to latency in audio transmission and bandwidth requirements in video transmission)

- GPS receiver

- Compass and acceleration sensor; these sensors are required together with the GPS receiver for realisation of AR

4.1.2. Requirements of the administration/monitoring tool

The administration/monitoring tool should be located on a website to support the caregiver's mobility and to be able to use the tool independently of an operating system. Table 4.2 shows the requirements of the administration/monitoring tool.

No	Function	Description	Support
1	Multi-User-Support	Multiple dementia patients should be able to be supported simultaneously	(++)
2	Administer routes	Caregivers can add, delete, stop or start routes for dementia patients	(++)
3	Every route for one weekday only	One weekday should be defined for each route, so that the route is repeated on a weekly basis	(+)
4	Name and point in time for route point	The route consists of route points with names and time points	(+)
5	Search for address	The address of every route point should be able to be searched	(+)
6	Monitoring	Caregiver should be able to see on a map where the patient is	(++)
7	Communication	Dementia patients should be able to communicate with caregivers via a website	(++)

Table 4.2.: Requirements of the administration/monitoring tool

To enable the caregiver to detect the dementia patient's position, GPS position data, heading data and video data from the mobile device should be displayed. The data should be sufficient to display the same environment to the caregiver that the dementia patient (or more precisely, the mobile phone) is currently viewing (or recording). As an additional aid, the Google Street View should be usable so that the location of the dementia patient can be accurately determined. The next chapter describes the technologies selected for the realisation of the system.

4.2. Technology selection

4.2.1. Augmented Reality

Augmented Reality (AR) is understood to be the extension of the reality surrounding the user by means of virtual elements in real time. AR is an extended development of virtual reality with the goal of improving the user's perception of reality, whereby reality – by contrast to Augmented Virtuality – is the focal point and is supplemented by additional information and virtual objects. A significant strength of AR is the intuitive representation of information, whereby the virtual and real objects coexist within the same sphere. The user can recognise required information, without having to understand abstract, textual metaphors. AR extends the perceptual capability of the user in the real world and provides support in interaction with objects in that information that cannot be determined by the user himself is presented.[2] According to Azuma[3], AR technologies should contain the following characteristics:

- Combination of reality and virtuality
- Interaction in real time
- Presentation of objects in 3D

With the aid of AR, an attempt is made to improve the environment visually perceived by individuals in terms of information content and understandibility by means of computer-generated, artificial objects. According to the definition, this occurs by overlaying corresponding objects in real time and by placing the user in a three-dimensional environment.

The AR research field is becoming increasingly significant in various areas of life. AR technology is widely used by the military, for example, with the aim of supporting soldiers with visual information in urban areas. Although AR has been researched for many years, more specifically since the middle of the 60s, it has been the focus of more intensive research in the last few years. This is linked to the constant increase in capability of mobile devices and the additional sensors with which they are equipped, which allow for AR. The potential for AR is immense, in the first instance with reference to mobile phones. Navigation is considered to be the primary area of use for AR in mobile phones. Modern mobile phones fulfil all requirements for AR: computing power, graphics functions, low weight and size, and various sensors.

[2]Izkara, J. L. (2008)
[3]Azuma, R. T. (1997)
[4][Web/UIUC]

AR has a relatively long history. The development of a system by Ivan Sutherland in 1968 that „convinced the human senses using virtual experiences"[5] can be seen as the birth of AR. In his study „The Ultimate Display" Sutherland describes the vision of virtual reality as „A display linked to a computer that offers us the option of realising concepts that cannot be realised in the real world. It is a magical mirror into a mathematical wonderland".[6] The next step was the Head Mounted Display (HMD) that generated frames and presented them in a display. However, the HMD was so heavy that it could not be worn on the head and consequently needed to be attached.

Figure 4.1.: Head Mounted Display[4]

Numerous research projects in the area of AR were started by different countries for the purposes of researching potential areas of use.[7]

The following main components for the realisation of an AR system can be listed:

- Display device
- Tracking system
- Hardware and software for scene generation

To provide information in the user's field of vision in real time, it is necessary to capture and determine the user's angle of vision and the distance between the user and the viewed (virtual) object or the (virtual) object to be viewed.

Based on this information, the real world can be extended using virtual objects at the correct positions. Capturing this data and transmitting it to the scene generator is the task of a tracking system.

---

[5]Tönnis, M. (2010) p. 3
[6]Sutherland, I. (1965)
[7]ISMR - International Symposium on Mixed Reality, Japan;
IWAR - IEEEWorkshop on Augmented Reality, USA;
ARVIKA Projekt, EU/Deutschland;
[8]Cawood, S. (2008)

The tracking system can be seen as one of the central technical focal points in AR systems. The accuracy of the object to be extended in reality depends on the information supplied by the tracking system.

The scene generator requires information as to the exact position where the digital image is to be extended. This data is usually obtained with the assistance of AR markers (marker-based systems). Different forms of markers (LED, human hand) are used. The simplest form of marker, however, is the unique pattern visible to

Figure 4.2.: The virtual fish[8]

the AR camera and that can be identified in the AR software using (frame) image analysis. The pattern is physically added to the real world, and every image contains AR tags. Figure 4.2 shows a virtual 3D fish and a pattern for tracking. The camera angle and the position of the object are determined using the AR tag. This data can be used to correctly position the virtual fish in reality. The disadvantage of this tracking system is that no calculations can be made from the real world without the assistance of the AR markers.

Another option for determining the exact position of the virtual object is the so-called Hybrid AR Tracking System. This tracking system uses the data supplied by the GPS receiver, the acceleration sensor/gyroscope and the compass. Figure 4.3 shows how various data can be or must be captured for this purpose. The angle of vision to the virtual object (vertical and horizontal) and the distance between the user and the virtual object can be calculated using the data. This data is sufficient to show the virtual object at its correct position and with the correct angles of vision on the display. The advantage of a hybrid tracking system such as this is that no AR markers are needed and that it functions anywhere in the world. This system has the potential to achieve sustainability, economy and improved quality in this sector. However, when using GPS, note should generally be taken that reception of the GPS signal can be affected by external influences such as mirror effects or metallic objects. The most decisive factor in this regard is the visibility of the satellites,[9] that is, the GPS receiver can only be used outdoors. An additional problem, however, is also that the update rate of the GPS signal is around 1-5 Hz, and the accuracy of measurement is not always satisfactory.

---

[9]Staub, G. M. (2006)

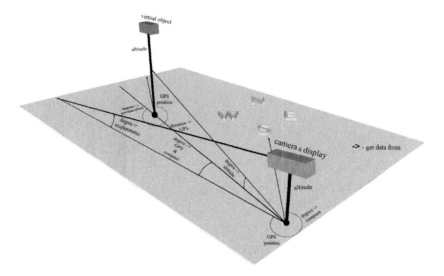

Figure 4.3.: The hybrid tracking system

4.2.2. Navigation

This term is derived from the Latin „navigatio", meaning ship travel in general. The word is used to mean the determination of the location in one place and the path from a starting point to a destination. An additional task of navigation is the optimisation of speed or reaction to unforeseen situations.[10]

At an early stage of history, humans discovered the need for navigation. Whether for conducting trade, settling new lands or researching foreign cultures, the need has always existed for navigating from one location to another. In time, and with the development of technology, navigation methods have improved. Although no clear distinction between navigation methods is possible,[11] the following can be listed:

- Terrestrial navigation: Determination of positions with the assistance of landmarks, radio beacons and maritime signals. Here the intersection of two baselines normally determines the current position

---

[10]Staub, G. M. (2006)
[11]Schlender, D. (2008) p. 8

- Sight navigation: Based on the comparison of suitable, accompanying map material and the observed landscape

- Dead reckoning: Location by means of continuous measurement of course, speed and time

- Astronomic navigation: Determination of position by observation of heavenly bodies (sun, moon, planets or stars)

- Radio navigation

    - Satellite navigation

- Inertial navigation

- Hybrid navigation

In 1862, the British physicist James Clerk Maxwell observed that electrical and magnetic fields could be linked to form progressive waves.[12] Guerlielmo Marconi and Ferdinand Braun researched a method for using these waves for wireless transmission of messages. Radio technology was used later for determining position. Radio navigation is the use of radio waves for determining position. In this regard, a distinction is made between bearing by a radio-compass station (VDF, radar: direction and/or location determination by means of devices installed on the ground) and aircraft-to-station bearing (ADF, GPS: on-board devices determine the direction and/or location).

Today, modern procedures are used for determining position: Satellite navigation or position determination using WLAN in closed areas. The position of the peer is determined by evaluating the signal strength between the access points and peers.[13]

Satellite navigation is part of radio navigation, as it also deals with a combination of transmission and receipt of radio waves.[14] Currently, two systems exits: the US NAVSTAR GPS and the Russian GLONASS (Global Navigation Satellite System). The systems are developed and operated by the Ministries of Defence of the USA and Russia respectively. The European Galileo system, the Chinese Beidou and the Indian IRNSS (Indian Regional Navigation Satellite System) are currently still in the development phase, although Beidou and IRNSS will only cover the territories of China and India respectively.

---

[12]Waalkes, J. (2011) p. 3
[13]Staub, G. M. (2006)
[14]Staub, G. M. (2006)
[15][Web/GoGo]

The US GPS consists of three components, the space, control and user segments. The space segment forms the core element of the navigation system, and consists of 24 satellites that orbit the earth in six paths twice per day at an altitude of approx. 20,200 km. These satellites are arranged in such a manner that GPS receivers anywhere on the earth's surface are accessible from at least 4 satellites at

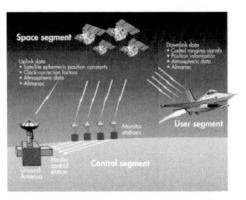

Figure 4.4.: Three segments of GPS[15]

any point in time. The task of the control segment is to direct the satellites. This includes the task of keeping the satellites in the correct orbits and monitoring their status. Five ground stations are located on the earth's surface. The user-segment (GPS receiver) receives signals from the satellites. After decryption, these signals deliver identification data (information via satellites), time and position data.

GPS is the only fully functional satellite navigation system and is the most widely distributed system for position determination. The location precision is constantly being improved, and is today of the order of 10 metres on the horizontal level with good satellite visibility and when using correction algorithms.[16] In the USA, the European Union, Canada, Japan, China and India stations such as WAAS, EGNOS, MSAS etc. enable location precision to be improved to 1 - 2 m[17].

GPS was originally developed to guide bombs, aircraft, soldiers and ships. In all cases, the expectation was that there would be visible contact between the GPS receiver and the satellite. It was expected that the startup time would be approx. one minute, and that operation thereafter would be continuous. Today, GPS is used for significantly more civilian applications than military. Expectations of today's systems include functionality of the GPS receiver everywhere, including indoors in some cases, and quick and efficient determination of the location. GPS alone cannot fulfil these requirements. To be able to do so (in particular as regards startup time), hybrid navigation, or aGPS (assisted GPS), was developed.

---

[16][Web/WAAS]
[17][Web/WAAS]

aGPS improves GPS output by using an alternative communications channel to make available information that the GPS receiver should normally have received from the satellite itself. aGPS therefore does not replace GPS, it complements it, making position determination easier and minimising the effort in terms of time required and the information needed for the satellites. The aGPS receiver still calculates the position based on data from satellites, but is able to do so much more quickly and with weaker signals. In the case of mobile phones, the radio network is used as a communications channel[18] that supplies information via satellite frequencies used by the GPS receiver.[19] This means that the startup time can be reduced from one minute to one second.[20]

[18]Diggelen, F. v. (2009) p. 227
[19]Diggelen, F. v. (2009) p. 2
[20]Diggelen, F. v. (2009) p. 3

4.2.3. Voice over IP

The advent of internet technology and high-speed data connectivity has seen the establishment of new telephony technologies. En route to a globalised world, VoIP (Voice over Internet Protocol) has considerable attraction both for companies or service providers, as well as for private users who use the internet as an inexpensive communications option. VoIP technology is primarily used by companies, which are then able to achieve the goal of reducing costs and increasing productivity.

In the 1990s, VoIP was used as a method for remote conversations with the aid of a computer and a microphone and headphones. Today however, the forms of use are much more extensive. The advantage that VoIP can replace or extend existing telephone systems without the need for converting to new communications systems has accelerated the implementation of this technology for telecommunication. Although VoIP offers transmission of digital audio packets, telephony can be both analogue and digital. Digital audio packets are converted into analogue form and vice versa with the assistance of VoIP gateway.

From a technical perspective, the internet is, strictly speaking, not necessary for VoIP. The same products should be used for the realisation of VoIP technology. VoIP can also be implemented in local networks via LAN or WLAN.

The quality of VoIP calls is dependent on various factors, including voice codecs, packaging, latency, jitter (latency fluctuations) and network architecture for ensuring QoS (Quality of Service). Other factors for successful VoIP calling are CAC (Call Admission Control), a security design, and NAT and firewall traversal.[21]

Package loss influences speech quality. Some voice codecs can correct lost packets. To ensure that the correction algorithm is effective, only one packet can be lost in a short period of time. Higher latency influences speech quality. The buffer compensates latency fluctuations in the receiving device. If the fluctuations are greater than the buffer, the buffer becomes empty. The result is similar to that in packet loss.

VoIP protocols can be used for audio conversations as well as for text[22] and video conversations. Audio and video data is converted into transmittable forms using codecs.

The use of voice codecs with lower network bandwidths leads to packet delay due to coding complexity. As a result, a compromise must be reached between packaging delay, coding

---

[21]For SIP and H.323, not for IAX
[22]Possible using SIP protocol

complexity and the requirements of the transmission capacity. To increase bandwidth efficiency, techniques such as speech pause recognition and silence suppression are used.

Many codecs are available for digitisation of speech. The most widely used VoIP voice codec is the guideline of the ITU (International Telecommunication Union) - G.711(A and μ[23]). This voice codec is digitised using the PCM algorithm and requires network bandwidths in the range of 64 Kb/s[24], without 31 Kbit/s overhead.

Another widely used voice codec is iLBC (internet Low Bitrate Codec). This codec was developed by Global IP Solutions and enables good speech quality in a network with low speed and with packet losses; iLBC requires 13.33 Kb/s at 30 ms frame or 15.2 Kb/s at 20 ms frame, plus 31 Kbit/s overhead.

The delay between sender and receiver is calculated as the sum of the coding (encoding and decoding) and transport time. A delay under 150 ms is not necessarily noticeable, between 150 ms and 300 ms is acceptable,[25] over 300 ms is unacceptable. The latency and jitter depend on network quality and stability. Latency values and jitter are particularly important in long-distance calls.

For better latency values, RTP/UDP/IP is typically used instead of TCP/IP for transmission in VoIP. TCP/IP is a reliable protocol that guarantees packet receipt using confirmations (ACK). This advantage of TCP in real-time communication is not usable, as ACK would lead to delays. In addition it would be pointless to resend packets lost in real-time communication; confirmation of packet receipt is consequently unnecessary.

The UDP is an unreliable, connectionless network protocol for transporting messages between end points. RTP is used together with UDP for transmission of real-time data such as audio and video. RTP does not reserve resources and guarantees QoS. Nevertheless, RTP/UDP/IP is used for transmission, without taking into consideration packet loss or latency.

The setup, monitoring or where necessary the deletion of media channels is known as „Call Signaling Protocols". The most important „Call Signalling Protocols" are Session Initiation Protocol (SIP), developed by Internet Engineering Task Force (IETF) and H.323, developed by ITU. Other protocols, such as Skinny Client Control Protocol (SCCP) from Cisco, UNISTIM from Nortel and IAX from Digium have been developed by private companies and contain only some of the functions that were missing from the first two. The main advantage of IAX in

---

[23]G.711A in Europe; G.711μ North America and Japan
[24]Every 125μs(8000Hz) an 8-bit sampling of the audio signal is generated: 8000 Hz x 8 bits = 64Kbit/s
[25]Cisco Systems states that a latency value of over 150 ms is unacceptable

comparison to SIP and H.323 is overhead, whereby communication over small bandwidths is made possible.

The SIP and H.323 protocols have been in development since the start of the 1990s. The main difference between SIP and H.323 is that the H.323 protocol contains communication via the traditional fixed network. By contrast, SIP was developed for point-to-point communication, that is, for SIP-internal communication only. However, by using additional hardware, (SIP/PSTN gateway), SIP can also be used as point-to-fixed network. In addition, implementation of the H.323 protocol is complex. IT experts praise the SIP protocol for its lack of errors and extensibility, when compared to the H.323 protocol. SIP is not only an audio and video telephony protocol, it is also open for all types of message-based applications.SIP uses a human-readable header, which is not the case for H.323.

SIP endpoint - SIP server - SIP endpoint communicate for the connection setup using so-called SIP methods. In so doing, the SIP endpoint can register at the SIP server using the REGISTER method, for example. Using the INVITE method, a different SIP endpoint can be invited to setup communication. Figure 4.5 shows how the SIP endpoints communicate with one another.

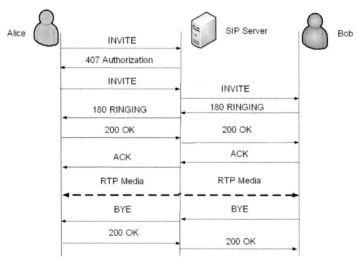

Figure 4.5.: Communication connection setup using SIP[26]

---
[26][Web/HI-Tech]

The SIP server consists of a DB server that collects and stores SIP endpoint information as to how individual SIP endpoints can be reached, namely from a SIP registrar and a SIP proxy. Each SIP endpoint registers with its SIP provider.[27] A SIP registrar is responsible for this task. The SIP endpoint can be reached as a URI:

$$sip:user@sip.example.com^{28}$$

Multiple SIP endpoints can be registered under a single URI, and all SIP endpoints will ring when an incoming call is detected.

If the SIP endpoints are not registered at the same SIP registrar, it is the task of the SIP proxy to forward the SIP endpoint connection request to the SIP proxy of the other SIP endpoint.

Session Description Protocol (SDP) is used for the description of the multimedia session. SDP mediates the messages between the SIP endpoints as to which audio and video coding is to be used to send data to which UDP ports.

SIP and H.323 are the largest competing IP telephony protocols, although in the long term, SIP is seen as the favourite for the future.[29] Even today, there are more SIP telephones in the world than H.323 telephones.

---

[27] Registration via TCP/IP

[28] *sip* - Protocol(*sips* for encrypted connection with TLS); *sip.example.com* - SIP-Registar; *user* - username

[29] [Web/H.323 vs. SIP]

4.2.4. Google Maps

Google Maps is a free[30] service from Google that offers high-performance, user-friendly maps as well as information on local companies and services.[31] The service contains maps and satellite images of the entire world (but also of the moon and Mars). Google Maps is being made available for a growing number of countries. This Google service is well developed for North America and Europe. It can be used to search for and then display addresses or POI anywhere in the world on a map. In addition, Google Maps offers a route planner for many countries – for vehicles, pedestrians and cyclists.

In 2007 Google added a new technology in the form of Google Street View. This technology makes available $360°$ panorama images from a street perspective. Google Street View is a three-dimensional representation of street images, which has been combined with a two-dimensional map. These images were created using special cars, bicycles and snowmobiles equipped with cameras and GPS receivers. Since its availability, Google Street View has been criticised for invading privacy. Google developed software to make people's faces and vehicle licence plates unrecognisable. Despite this, protection of privacy has not been sufficiently assured, as people can be recognised without their faces being visible.

The satellite images of the world were first made available by Google in Google Earth. Later, these images could be called up from a web browser. Now, they are also supported on mobile platforms such as Android, iOS, Symbian, Windows Mobile etc. As almost all modern mobile phones are equipped with a built-in GPS receiver, and have an internet connection, a service such as this is extremely significant.

---

[30]Under Google licence conditions
[31][Web/GMaps]

4.2.5. Apple iPhone

The iPhone product encompasses a range of multimedia smartphones manufactured by Apple Inc. The smartphone combines the functions of a mobile phone, a multimedia player and the option for internet connectivity in a single device. The first iPhone became available in 2007, and captured the largest share of the mobile phone market in the USA. The following versions of the iPhone range were equipped with an aGPS receiver, magnetometer (digital compass), gyroscope and HD camera. The latest iPhone 4S has a dual-core Apple A5 processor with 1 GHz computing power per core and 512 MB RAM. The iPhone has a multi-touch screen with a resolution of 960 x 640. 3G technology has been supported from the iPhone 3G, allowing surfing speeds of up to 7,200 Kb/s and better latency. According to Apple, the battery has a life of 200 hours in standby mode (300 hours for iPhone 4), and 6 hours when performing 3G internet surfing.

The iPhone contains a simplified, optimised version of the Mac OS X operating system, iOS, together with a Darwin kernel, and is similar to UNIX. A wide range of frameworks are available in iOS. Developers can write applications in C, C++ and Objective-C.

With reference to persons affected by dementia, a special device would be the wrong decision, due to the feeling of shame experienced by dementia patients. Modern smartphones, such as iPhones or mobile phones based on Android, already fulfil the hardware requirements of this study, with one exception. In some cases, the advantage of a touchscreen for healthy individuals could be a disadvantage for dementia patients, as they can suffer from deficits in hand motor functioning. Another important point is that the unavailability of buttons can be just as confusing as too many buttons for a dementia patient. The evaluation is intended to show whether an iPhone can be used by a dementia patient, despite the fact that the phone will only have one button. Other hardware requirements, such as 3G internet technology, an aGPS receiver, compass and an acceleration sensor are fulfilled by the iPhone, for example.

Mobile phones with Android fulfil the hardware requirements just as well as the iPhone. The tool can therefore be developed for these mobile phones as well. I have decided to develop the first prototype of the tool for the iPhone, as this phone has a wider range of available frameworks and developed applications. In addition, the iPhone operating system is more stable. The iPhone is also better documented, and many people find the device extremely appealing.

5. Realisation

The system consists of two parts: the administration/monitoring web application, which is installed on a website, and the reminder/navigation application on the iPhone. The application on the iPhone creates a connection to the web server. This data determines the behaviour of the iPhone application.

The first step in using the system is the administration of routes. All functions of the two applications are explained below.

Figure 5.1 shows the website on which the routes can be administered. The website uses Google Maps JavaScript API V3 for displaying the map with the polyline and the position of the user for searching addresses or POI.

The Google Maps service provides an option for automatically calculating and displaying the route between two addresses for pedestrians, vehicle drivers or cyclists. The route consists of route points that are connected to one another. Every route point is a position on the map with geographical latitude and longitude values. The route points calculated by Google are not always correct. For example, the route points are sometimes set in such a manner that a street must be crossed several times, or the route travels through areas that are not accessible to pedestrians. Hagethorn and Kröse[1] report dangerous behaviour of dementia patients who attempt to cross a street using a navigation aid, without looking out for vehicles. As the route points from Google are imprecise, dementia patients can be exposed to danger. This means that the route points on the route must be manually entered.

The website was set up using PHP. MySQL DB was used as a database. AJAX technology was used for the administration tool and for the monitoring tool, so that the current data can be loaded without having to reload the entire page.

---

[1] Hagethorn, F. N. (2008)

Figure 5.1.: Administration tool

Table 5.1 describes the functions provided, and shown in Figure 5.1.

No	Function	Description
1	Search, add marker	To add a route point, an address or POI can be searched for; if the search is successful, a marker (route point) is added. Markers can also be added on the map by clicking on a particular point on the map using the mouse.
2	Describe marker	After at least two markers have been added, start and end points must be added for the first and last markers respectively. For markers between the first and last markers, information describing the marker can be added. Input errors are detected by the system and are noted in yellow.
3	Add route	After the route points have been edited, the route can be stored in the database. For this, the name of the route and the day of the week must be entered for the route. Based on the details relating to day of the week and marker time, the system responds to a query from the navigation tool as to which route must be followed. The routes added are listed under the map.
4	Delete marker	Markers that have been added to the map but not yet stored can be deleted.
5	Move marker	Every marker can be moved to a new point. A marker must first be activated before it can be moved. The marker can be activated by clicking on an inactive marker using the mouse.
6	Delete route	The routes added can be deleted from the database.
7	Start/stop route	It is conceivable that an existing route should not be followed on a weekday as an exception, for example on a public holiday. In a situation such as this, individual routes can be stopped without being deleted.
-	Change or display existing route	Click on an existing route to display the route on the map. To change the route, the route must be displayed, modified and then added as a new route. The old route must then be deleted.

Table 5.1.: Functions of the administration tool

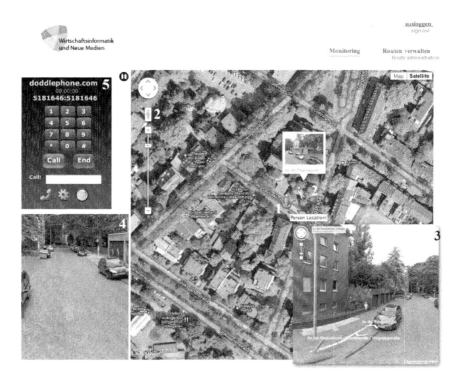

Figure 5.2.: Monitoring tool

Figure 5.2 shows the monitoring tool and its functions. The tool consists of three main sections: map, video stream from the user's mobile phone and the Java Applet SIP tool. The marker is used to display the user's position, direction in which the mobile phone is being held as well as the polyline (route). To support the caregiver, the Google Street View Service is alsoprovided, which is intended to simplify his task, in combination with the video stream from the user's mobile phone. The user's position is also displayed on the Street View image using the marker.[2] Google Street View is not available everywhere, however.

To enable communication between dementia patients and caregivers, Doodle's Java Applet

---

[2]In Google Maps JavaScript API V3 it is only possible to show the polyline on the map, not in Google Street View

SIP tool was integrated in the page[3]. The SIP account data must be entered in the database manually. Where a browser that is not Java compatible is used, or where no browser exists, the SIP provider's call-forwarding function can be used to route calls to the caregiver's mobile phone. Another option for receiving calls is to use a separate SIP application, such as the free X-Lite SIP tool. Finally, an option exists for setting the SIP account directly in a VoIP-capable DSL modem.

The reminder/navigation tool reminds the user that he should now depart, and assists him in orienting himself. In passive mode, the tool sends a query to the server every minute. The server responds with the route data, which was entered with the assistance of the administration tool. The data is sent from the server at the latest 15 minutes earlier than the first route point needs to be passed. Even when an active route exists that has been received by the server, the tool forwards the query to the server. A check is also performed as to whether the route was stopped or deleted. By means of this combination, the tool can react to the user's changes in one minute at the latest. Once a new route has been loaded, an acoustic signal is issued, informing the user that a new route has been received, which must be confirmed. The message is repeated until receipt of the route is confirmed (see image **b** in Figure 5.3).

The battery life is an important topic where a tool is developed for a mobile device. According to Apple, the battery life of an iPhone with 3G internet usage is six hours. However, tests have shown that the battery lasts for up to 4.5 hours[4] only if the developed tool is active (see images **b** and **c** in Figure 5.3). This relates to the fact that besides 3G internet, the tool also uses data from the GPS receiver, the magnetometer (compass), acceleration sensor and camera. The AR real-time calculations also drain the battery. To drain the battery as little as possible, all sensors and the camera are switched off and the background switched to black[5] in passive mode, if no route is to be followed (see image **a** in Figure 5.3). In passive mode, the iPhone can remain on for up to 12 hours. To be able to meet the requirement that dementia patients can phone the caregiver at any time, the tool must be in foreground mode.

Figure 5.4 shows the settings. Firstly, the domain, username and password of the HTTP server, and the SIP settings and the caregiver's number must be entered. For IP telephony on the iPhone, Liblinphone VoIP SDK was used.

---

[3] The iLBC codec is unfortunately not supported. This codec is more suitable for calls on the mobile internet
[4] If audio, video and position data is sent to the server, that is, when the call button is activated, a discharge time of 3.5 hours must be factored in;
all values are in normal display brightness
[5] Black pixel uses the least current

| a) Waiting | b) Confirm new route | c) Follow arrow |

Figure 5.3.: The reminder/navigation tool

Figure 5.4.: Tool settings

An option exists to always send the GPS position data to the caregiver. If the dementia patient is 36 metres from the route, or if the route point has not been passed at the latest by the time entered, the user receives an acoustic notification that he should call the caregiver if he is uncertain as to where he is. If an automatic call is ticked in the settings, the tool automatically calls the caregiver. If the call button is pressed, the position, compass and video data are sent.

As dementia patients show deficits in hand motor skills as the illness progresses, the number of touches on the screen needed to start the tool was reduced. To do this, the iPhone's operating system was modified. By pressing the Home button on the iPhone, the phone is unlocked and the navigation tool is started. In addition, the text and the size of the application icons were increased as the user of the tool is often at an advanced age and possibly has reduced visual acuity.

Suggestions for improvement are discussed before the evaluation. The system could improve some functions. These changes could be implemented in further prototypes. Hetting[6], de Boer[7] and Nakamura[8] report that people with dementia respond better to a known person's voice in the case of an acoustic notification. This function could also be implemented in the next prototypes. Technical improvements could include improvements to the physics of the AR objects.

[6]Hetting, M. (2009)
[7]Boer de, J. (2008)
[8]Nakamura, K. (2001)

6. Evaluation

This chapter describes the methodology and process for evaluation of the prototype of the system developed. The chapter concludes with an analysis of the results of the evaluation

6.1. Methodology and process

When evaluating the navigation system prototype created, results should be collected more precisely with special reference to the research questions and the usability of the prototype. To be able to answer these questions, detailed questions that refer directly to the functions of the navigation system were designed.

After the functions of the system were explained to caregivers and dementia patients, suggestions for improvement were requested. Thereafter, the system was used together with the caregivers and the dementia sufferers. In this process, dementia patients and caregivers were observed in order to identify the weak points of the system. The results are described in detail below.

6.2. Results

As already mentioned in previous chapters, all dementia patients interviewed (with one exception) were at an advanced age and were in a state of health that made them completely unable to go walking without an accompanying person due to their age and illness. The dementia patients' caregivers were required to have basic skills in using a computer and the internet to be able to use the system. For these reasons, the evaluation was only conducted with one dementia patient and caregiver. Some functions of the system were considered together with the users. The general system evaluation results are listed below in the analysis and evaluation of the results.

Overall, the dementia patient and the caregiver found the system and individual functions to be extremely helpful. Despite the deficits in hand motor skills, the dementia patient was able to use the application on the iPhone without difficulty, to use the call button and to reduce or enlarge the map using a double-touch on the screen. Due to the deficits in hand motor skills, a device such as an iPhone can easily slip out of the hand and be damaged. The advantage of Augmented Reality Navigation as opposed to map-based and landmark-based navigation was immediately recognisable. The user found it extremely easy to simply follow one arrow without having to orient himself to the map. The caregiver expressed the wish that the acoustic notifications describe the actions in more detail. This can be implemented by adding a separate notification[1] for individual route points on the route.

However, there are also technical limitations that prevent full use of the system developed, particularly during remote-controlled support. Some of these questions have been described in the chapters on technology selection and implementation. Mobile internet speed differs from one location to another. In many cases, this speed is insufficient for simultaneous transmission of video and audio data. The operating system architecture of the iPhone does not permit integration of calling functions into the application, so that it is necessary to transmit audio data via mobile wireless telephony rather than via the internet. This leads to the problem that the quality of the phone conversation via mobile internet is not always sufficiently high.

An additional related problem is that the maps provided by Google Maps for some locations are out of date. For this reason, it is sometimes complicated to add the route points at the right locations of the map.

It would also be desirable if the application were to respond appropriately to acoustic commands from the user in emergency situations, such as „Take me home" (or also „Where am I?"). However, implementing this is not yet a trivial task.[2] A function such as this would increase the dementia patient's feeling of independence and take the load off the caregiver.

---

[1] In the prototype I created, the notifications were not route-dependent;
the notifications were the same for all routes, depending on the user's position
[2] Using Siri SDK (if this is made available) and improved Google Navigation, this can definitely be implemented for pedestrians

7. Summary

Advances in medicine and the increasing quality of life contribute to an increase in life expectancy across the world. As a result, the number of dementia patients is increasing. At the age of 90, 35% of individuals suffer from dementia. The most common form of dementia is Alzheimer's disease. There is no cure for dementia. However, scientists hope to be able to impede the progress of dementia. Support and care of dementia patients is extremely cost-intensive for the state. These costs will rise in the future.

To increase the safety, freedom and feeling of self-worth of dementia patients, but also to reduce costs of care and support, different systems have been developed. To a large extent, these systems are intended for patients in the advanced stages of dementia. There are tracking systems that can be used to locate dementia patients if they stray, as well as systems for monitoring everyday activities and the intake of medication for dementia patients at home.

Individuals can suffer from the early stages of dementia for eight to nine years before the dementia is so advanced that the patient cannot survive without external assistance. Navigation systems that assist in orientation have also been developed for early-stage dementia patients. Many studies have reported the success of landmark-based navigation systems by contrast to map-based ones. The use of AR technology for navigation systems for dementia patients has not been researched up till now.

The studies by Marquardt and Hagethorn describe general requirements of systems to be developed for dementia patients. The most important insights were that the tool should be usable without having to acquire new skills and that the decision making should be reduced to the minimum. Furthermore, it was established that people respond better to acoustic notifications rather than visual ones such as texts.

The results of the preliminary study confirmed a great deal of the prior knowledge from the research fields as to dementia and the problems of dementia patients. The most important finding was that a navigation system without a reminder function for dementia patients, which was partially considered in some studies in the research fields, would not be used in a real-world situation. Dementia patients can forget what they should do in order to be helped. For this reason, patients should be reminded in emergency situations. This is also a finding derived from the preliminary study.

The system was developed for the iPhone, based on prior knowledge from the research fields and the preliminary study, and is administered via a website. The website also provides functions for monitoring.

In the course of the evaluation, problems of a technical nature in particular were determined, such as the mobile internet speed problem. However, the evaluation could only be performed with one dementia patient. In future studies, evaluation should be performed on more patients over a longer period of time.

Bibliography

[1] ARMSTRONG, NICOLA; NUGENT, CHRIS: *Mapping User Needs to Smartphone Services for Persons with Chronic Disease*, 2009
http://www.springerlink.com/content/2378226k61v37817/
Date last accessed on Friday 19th August, 2011

[2] AZUMA, RONALD T.: *A Survey of Augmented Reality*, 1997
http://www.cs.unc.edu/~azuma/ARpresence.pdf
Date last accessed on Sunday 2nd October, 2011

[3] BEIGL, MICHAEL: *MemoClip: A Location-Based Remembrance Appliance*, 2006
http://www.springerlink.com/content/t84027784x138511/
Date last accessed on Thursday 11th August, 2011

[4] BIMBER, OLIVER: *Interactive Rendering For Projection-Based Augmented Reality Displays*, 2002
http://tuprints.ulb.tu-darmstadt.de/270/
Date last accessed on Friday 2nd September, 2011

[5] BISWAS, JIT; MOKHTAR, MOUNIR: *Mild Dementia Care at Home - Integrating Activity Monitoring, User Interface Plasticity and Scenario Verification*, 2010
http://www.springerlink.com/content/h0q13x222u302274/
Date last accessed on Friday 2nd September, 2011

[6] BLACKMAN, TIM; VAN SCHAIK, PAUL: *Outdoor Environments for People With Dementia: An Exploratory Study Using Virtual Reality*, 2007
http://journals.cambridge.org/production/action/cjoGetFulltext?
fulltextid=1399092
Date last accessed on Monday 5th September, 2011

[7] BOER DE, JOHANNES: *Auditory Navigation for Persons with Mild Dementia*, 2008
http://essay.utwente.nl/58461/
Date last accessed on Tuesday 12th July, 2011

[8] CAWOOD, STEPHEN; FIALA, MARK: *Augmented Reality: A Practical Guide*. 1st
edition, Pragmatic Bookshelf, Wien, 2008

[9] CARMICHAEL, ALEX; RICE, MARK; LINDSAY, STEPHEN; OLIVIER, PATRICK: *iTV
as a Platform for Rich Multimedia Reminders for People with Dementia*, 2008
http://www.springerlink.com/content/015082341131574v/
Date last accessed on Saturday 10th September, 2011

[10] CERNIGLIA, ANDREW J.: *Excerpts from: The Discovery of Grounded Theory:
Strategies for Qualitative Research by Barney G. Glaser and Anselm L. Strauss*, 2008
http://andrewcerniglia.com/documents/The_Discovery_of_Grounded_
Theory.pdf
Date last accessed on Saturday 20th August, 2011

[11] CHARMAZ, KATHY: *Constructing Grounded Theory: A Practical Guide Through Qualitative Analysis*. 2nd edition, SAGE Publications Ltd., London, 2010

[12] CHOUBASSI, MAHA EL; NESTARES, OSCAR; WU, YI: *An Augmented Reality Tourist
Guide on Your Mobile Devices*, 2010
http://www.springerlink.com/content/l1805wk322748300/
Date last accessed on Saturday 10th September, 2011

[13] DALE, ØYSTEIN: *Usability and Usefulness of GPS Based Localization Technology Used
in Dementia Care*, 2010
http://www.springerlink.com/content/p655r41554p44551/
Date last accessed on Monday 1st August, 2011

[14] DIGGELEN, FRANK VAN: *A-GPS: Assisted GPS, GNSS, and SBAS*. Artech House,
Boston, 2009

[15] DRÖES, ROSE-MARIE; KNOOP, ELLEN C.C. BOESLENS-VAN DER; BOS, JOKE:
*Quality of Life In Dementia In Perspective: An Explorative Study of Variations in Opinions
Among People With Dementia And Their Professional Caregivers, And in Literature*, 2006
http://dem.sagepub.com/content/5/4/533.short
Date last accessed on Thursday 1st September, 2011

[16] DU, KEJUN; ZHANG, DAQING; ZHOU, XINGSHE: *HYCARE: A Hybrid Context-Aware Reminding Framework for Elders with Mild Dementia*, 2008
http://www.springerlink.com/content/r2263200rq555167/
Date last accessed on Saturday 10th September, 2011

[17] FISCHER, JÖRG: *VoIP-Praxisleitfaden: IP-Kommunikation für Sprache, Daten und Video planen, implementieren und betreiben*. Carl Hanser Verlag, München, 2008

[18] FOOK, VICTOR FOO SIANG; TEE, JHY HAUR; YAP, KON SANG: *Smart Mote-Based Medical System for Monitoring and Handling Medication Among Persons with Dementia*, 2007
http://www.springerlink.com/content/l07116t820g742t2/
Date last accessed on Friday 13th May, 2011

[19] FUDICKAR, SEBASTIAN; SCHNOR, BETTINA: *KopAL - A Mobile Orientation System for Dementia Patients*, 2009
http://www.springerlink.com/content/q031q5l186385720/
Date last accessed on Thursday 25th August, 2011

[20] FUDICKAR, SEBASTIAN; SCHNOR, BETTINA: *KopAL - Ein Orientierungssystem für demente Patienten*, 2011
http://www.telemed-initiative.de/konferenzen/5-fachkonferenz/
dokumente-5-landeskonferenz/vortrag-schnor
Date last accessed on Thursday 25th August, 2011

[21] GABBARD, JOSEPH L.; SWAN II, J. EDWARD: *Usability Engineering for Augmented Reality: Employing User-based Studies to Inform Design*, 2007
http://www.cse.msstate.edu/~swan/publications/papers/2008_
Gabbard-Swan_UE-AR_TVCG.pdf
Date last accessed on Saturday 13th August, 2011

[22] GATTERER, GERALD; CROY, ANTONIA: *Leben mit Demenz: Praxisbezogener Ratgeber für Pflege und Betreuung*. Springer Verlag, Wien, 2005

[23] GLÄSER, JOCHEN; LAUDEL, GRIT: *Experteninterviews und qualitative Inhaltsanalyse: als Instrumente rekonstruierender Untersuchungen*. 3. überarbeitete Auflage, VS Verlag, Wiesbaden, 2009

[24] GLASER, BARNEY; STRAUSS, ANSELM: *The Discovery of Grounded Theory: Strategies for Qualitative Research, Aldine*. 8th edition, Aldine Transaction, Chicago, 1977

[25] GOODMAN, J.; BREWSTER, S. (A): *Older People, Mobile Devices and Navigation*, 2004
http://www.dcs.gla.ac.uk/~stephen/research/utopia/workshop/goodman.pdf
Date last accessed on Friday 12th August, 2011

[26] GOODMAN, J.; BREWSTER, S. (B): *Using Field Experiments to Evaluate Mobile Guides*, 2004
http://citeseerx.ist.psu.edu/viewdoc/download?doi=10.1.1.100.3975&rep=rep1&type=pdf
Date last accessed on Friday 12th August, 2011

[27] GOODMAN, J.; BREWSTER, S. (C): *Using Landmarks to Support Older People in Navigation*, 2004
http://www.springerlink.com/content/6jj90tvrc06y6lyh/
Date last accessed on Friday 12th August, 2011

[28] GOODMAN, J.; BREWSTER, S. (D): *How Can We Best Use Landmarks to Support Older People in Navigation?*, 2005
http://www.dcs.gla.ac.uk/~stephen/papers/lr_3-20.pdf
Date last accessed on Friday 12th August, 2011

[29] GRIERSON, LAWRENCE E. M.; ZELEK, JOHN; LAM, ISABEL: *Application of a Tactile Way-Finding Device to Facilitate Navigation in Persons With Dementia*, 2011
http://www.tandfonline.com/doi/abs/10.1080/10400435.2011.567375
Date last accessed on Monday 22nd August, 2011

[30] HAGETHORN, F. N.; KRÖSE B. J. A.; DE GREEF , P.; HELMER, M. E.: *Creating Design Guidelines for a Navigational Aid for Mild Demented Pedestrians*, 2008
http://www.springerlink.com/content/327555234546m88u/
Date last accessed on Friday 12th August, 2011

[31] HANCOCK, GERALDINE A.; REYNOLDS, TOM; WOODS, BOB: *The Needs of Older People With Mental Health Problems According to the User, the Carer, And the Staff*, 2003
http://onlinelibrary.wiley.com/doi/10.1002/gps.924/abstract
Date last accessed on Thursday 1st September, 2011

[32] HENS, FRANCISCO J.; CABALLERO, JOSE M.: *Triple Plaz: Building the Converged Network for IP, VoIP and IPTV.* Wiley-VCH Verlag GmbH, Weinheim,, 2008

[33] HETTING, MARIKE; DE BOER, JOHANNES: *Navigation for People with Mild Dementia,* 2009
http://www.hst.aau.dk/~ska/MIE2009/papers/MIE2009p0428.pdf
Date last accessed on Friday 19th August, 2011

[34] HILE, HARLAN; VEDANTHAM, RAMAKRISHNA: *Landmark-Based Pedestrian Navigation from Collections of Geotagged Photos,* 2008
http://dl.acm.org/citation.cfm?id=1543167
Date last accessed on Friday 19th August, 2011

[35] HÖWLER, ELISABETH: *Gerontopsychiatrische Pflege: Lehr- und Arbeitsbuch für die Altenpflege.* 2. Auflage, Brigitte Kunz Verlag, Hannover, 2004

[36] IZKARA, JOSE LUIS; PEREZ, JUAN; BASOGAIN, XABIER: *Mobile Augmented Reality, an Advanced Tool for the Construction Sector,* 2008
http://citeseerx.ist.psu.edu/viewdoc/download?doi=10.1.1.113.3717&
rep=rep1&type=pdf
Date last accessed on Tuesday 12th July, 2011

[37] KAMINOYAMA, HIROKI; MATSUO, TAKASHI; HATTORI, FUMIO: *Walk Navigation System Using Photographs for People with Dementia,* 2007
http://www.springerlink.com/content/g4r0643gr827h744/
Date last accessed on Monday 22nd August, 2011

[38] KAPLAN, ELLIOTT D.; HEGARTY, CHRISTOPHER J.: *Understanding GPS: principles and applications.* 2nd Edition, Artech House, Nordwood, 2005

[39] KASTEREN, T. L. M. VAN; ENGLEBIENNE, G.; KRÖSE, B. J. A.: *An Activity Monitoring System for Ederly Care Using Generative and Discriminative Models,* 2010
http://www.springerlink.com/content/900556424771nm3r/
Date last accessed on Monday 22nd August, 2011

[40] KIM, SEUNGJUN; DEY, ANIND K.: *Simulated Augmented Reality Windshield Display as a Cognitive Mapping Aid for Elder Driver Navigation,* 2009
http://dl.acm.org/citation.cfm?id=1518724
Date last accessed on Monday 22nd August, 2011

67

[41] KROMREY, HELMUT: *Empirische Sozialforschung: Modelle und Methoden der standardisierten Datenerhebung und Datenauswertung.* 11. Auflage, UTB Verlag, Stuttgart, 2002

[42] LANDAUA, ALAN L.; AUSLANDERA, GAIL K.; WERNER, SHIRLI: *Who Should Make the Decision on the Use of GPS for People With Dementia?*, 2010
http://www.tandfonline.com/doi/abs/10.1080/13607861003713166
Date last accessed on Wednesday 10th August, 2011

[43] LIU, RUTH; HILE, HARLAN; BORRIELLO, GAETANO: *Informing the Design of an Automated Wayfinding System for Individuals with Cognitive Impairments*, 2009
http://citeseerx.ist.psu.edu/viewdoc/download?doi=10.1.1.156.5881&
rep=rep1&type=pdf
Date last accessed on Saturday 20th August, 2011

[44] LOU, RICARDO CASTELLOT; GIULIANO, ANGELE: *State of the Art in Electronic Assistive Technologies for People with Dementia*, 2010
http://www.springerlink.com/content/hg84138xm32g3532/
Date last accessed on Saturday 27th August, 2011

[45] MAILAND, F.J.M.; REINERSMANN, A.: *COGKNOW Development and Evaluation of an ICT-Device for People With Mild Dementia*, 2007
http://eprints.ulster.ac.uk/11525/
Date last accessed on Saturday 2nd July, 2011

[46] MARQUARDT, GESINE: *Wayfinding for People With Dementia: The Role of Architectural Design*, 2011
http://www.universalraum.de/download/Marquardt_2011.pdf
Date last accessed on Saturday 17th September, 2011

[47] MAY, ANDREW J.; ROSS, TRACY: *Pedestrian Navigation Aids: Information Requirements and Design Implications*, 2003
http://www.springerlink.com/content/7xvfdbug7ynbcap5/
Date last accessed on Wednesday 27th July, 2011

[48] MAYRING, PHILIPP: *Qualitative Inhaltsanalyse*, 2010
http://www.springerlink.com/content/q47737165886r5p8/
Date last accessed on Friday 15th July, 2011

[49] MEY, GÜNTER; MRUCK, KATJA: *Grounded Theory Reader.* 2. Auflage, Springer Verlag, Wiesbaden, 2011

[50] MISKELLY, FRANK: *A Novel System of Electronic Tagging in Patients With Dementia and Wandering*, 2004
http://ageing.oxfordjournals.org/content/33/3/304.abstract
Date last accessed on Friday 12th August, 2011

[51] MISKELLY, FRANK: *Electronic Tracking of Patients With Dementia and Wandering Using Mobile Phone Technology*, 2005
http://ageing.oxfordjournals.org/content/34/5/497.abstract
Date last accessed on Friday 12th August, 2011

[52] MULVENNA, MAURICE; MARTIN, SUZANNE; SÄVENSTEDT, STEFAN; BENGTSSON, JOHAN: *Designing and Evaluating a Cognitive Prosthetic for People with Mild Dementia*, 2010
http://dl.acm.org/citation.cfm?id=1962306
Date last accessed on Wednesday 11th May, 2011

[53] NAKAMURA, KATSUKI; KAWASHIMA, RYUTA; SUGIURA, MOTOAKI: *Neural Substrates for Recognition of Familiar Voices: a PET Study*, 2001
http://www.sciencedirect.com/science/article/pii/S0028393201000379/
Date last accessed on Thursday 1st September, 2011

[54] NARZT, WOLFGANG; POMBERGER, GUSTAV; FERSCHA, ALOIS: *A New Visualization Concept for Navigation Systems*, 2004
http://www.springerlink.com/content/f9xfwjda24r3puav/
Date last accessed on Thursday 1st September, 2011

[55] NARZT, WOLFGANG; POMBERGER, GUSTAV; FERSCHA, ALOIS: *Augmented Reality Navigation Systems*, 2005
http://www.springerlink.com/content/768802t64m428523/
Date last accessed on Thursday 1st September, 2011

[56] NUGENT, CHRIS; MULVENNA, MAURICE; MOELAERT, FERIAL: *Home Based Assistive Technologies for People with Mild Dementia*, 2007
http://www.springerlink.com/content/v110np1759486756/
Date last accessed on Friday 2nd September, 2011

[57] ROEST, HENRIËTTE G. VAN DER; MEILAND, FRANKA J. M.; MAROCCINI, RAFFAELLA: *Subjective Needs of People With Dementia: A Review of the Literature*, 2007
http://journals.cambridge.org/action/displayAbstract?fromPage=online&aid=1002168
Date last accessed on Thursday 1st September, 2011

[58] SAWANO, HIROAKI; OKADA, MINORU: *A Car-navigation System based on Augmented Reality*, 2005
http://dl.acm.org/citation.cfm?id=1187255
Date last accessed on Friday 5th August, 2011

[59] SCHEEHAN, BART; BURTON, ELIZABETH: *Outdoor Wayfinding in Dementia*, 2006
http://dem.sagepub.com/content/5/2/271.full.pdf+html
Date last accessed on Friday 5th August, 2011

[60] SCHLENDER, DIRK: *Multimediale Informationssysteme zum Vermitteln von kognitivem Navigationswissen* . Logos Verlag, Berlin, 2008

[61] SILVERMAN, DAVID: *Qualitative Research*. 3rd edition, SAGE Publications Ltd., London, 2011

[62] SOHN, TIMOTHY; LI, KEVIN A.; LEE, GUNNY: *Place-Its: A Study of Location-Based Reminders on Mobile Phones*, 2005
http://research.microsoft.com/apps/pubs/default.aspx?id=132415
Date last accessed on Wednesday 3rd August, 2011

[63] STAUB, GUIDO MARTIN: *Navigation mit mobilen Augmented Reality Systemen im Gelände*, 2006
http://digbib.ubka.uni-karlsruhe.de/volltexte/1000004871
Date last accessed on Friday 1st April, 2011

[64] SUTHERLAND, IVAN E.: *The Ultimate Display*, 1965
http://www.eng.utah.edu/~cs6360/Readings/UltimateDisplay.pdf
Date last accessed on Saturday 1st October, 2011

[65] TAYLOR, RICHARD: *Alzheimer und Ich: Leben mit Dr. Alzheimer im Kopf.* 1. Auflage, Huber Verlag, Göttingen, 2008

[66] TEGTMEIER, ANDRE: *Augmented Reality als Anwendungstechnologie in der Automobilindustrie*, 2006
http://diglib.uni-magdeburg.de/Dissertationen/2007/andtegtmeier.pdf
Date last accessed on Saturday 1st October, 2011

[67] TÖNNIS, MARCUS: *Augmented Reality: Einblicke in die Erweiterte Realität*. 1. Auflage, Springer Verlag, Berlin-Heidelberg, 2010

[68] THOMAS, BRUCE; CLOSE, BEN; DONOGHUE, JOHN: *First Person Indoor/Outdoor Augmented Reality Application: ARQuake*, 2002
http://www.springerlink.com/content/v9jf8xfg28cu1qfh/
Date last accessed on Monday 1st August, 2011

[69] VELDKAMP, D.; HAGETHORN, F.: *The Use of Visual landmarks in a Wayfinding System for Elderly with Beginning Dementia*, 2008
http://dare.uva.nl/document/118437
Date last accessed on Saturday 27th August, 2011

[70] VÖLKEL, THORSTEN; WEBER, GERHARD: *A New Approach for Pedestrian Navigation for Mobility Impaired Users Based on Multimodal Annotation of Geographical Data*, 2007
http://www.springerlink.com/content/44569w64467xk357/
Date last accessed on Monday 22nd August, 2011

[71] VÖLKEL, THORSTEN; KÜHN, ROMINA; WEBER, GERHARD : *Mobility Impaired Pedestrians Are Not Cars: Requirements for the Annotation of Geographical Data*, 2008
http://www.springerlink.com/content/r82160299q3p35r8/
Date last accessed on Sunday 11th September, 2011

[72] WAALKES, JAN: *Entwicklung der satellitengesteuerten Navigation in der Automobilindustrie*. Grin Verlag, München, 2011

[73] WALTHER-F., BENJAMIN; MALAKA, RAINER: *Evaluation of an Augmented Photograph-Based Pedestrian Navigation System*, 2008
http://www.springerlink.com/content/g8025g2452551216/
Date last accessed on Wednesday 11th May, 2011

[74] WALLINGFORD, THEODORE: *Switching to VoIP*. 1st Edition, O'Reilly, Sebastopol, 2005

71

[75] WEISSENBERGER, MONIQUE: *Palliativpflege bei Demenz: ein Handbuch für die Praxis.* 1. Auflage, Springer Verlag, Wiesbaden, 2009

[76] WINKLER, ISTVÁN; COWAN, NELSON: *From Sensory to Long-Term Memory: Evidence from Auditory Memory Reactivation Studies,* 2005
http://www.psycontent.com/content/gv8k3j1602710621/
Date last accessed on Thursday 1st September, 2011

[77] WITT, HARALD: *Forschungsstrategien bei quantitativer und qualitativer Sozialforschung,* 2001
http://www.qualitative-research.net/index.php/fqs/rt/printerFriendly/969/2114
Date last accessed on Sunday 21st August, 2011

[78] WHERTON, JOSEPH P.; MONK, ANDREW F.: *Technological Opportunities for Supporting People With Dementia Who are Living at Home,* 2008
http://dl.acm.org/citation.cfm?id=1379664
Date last accessed on Friday 2nd September, 2011

[79] [Web/AFI] Alzheimer Forschung Initiative: Diagnose
http://www.alzheimer-forschung.de/alzheimer-krankheit/faq.htm
Date last accessed on Saturday 6th August, 2011

[80] [Web/AZK] World Alzheimer Report 2010
http://www.alz.co.uk/research/world-report
Date last accessed on Tuesday 6th September, 2011

[81] [Web/CNN] GPS shoe to track Alzheimer's patients
http://edition.cnn.com/2009/HEALTH/06/10/gps.shoes/
Date last accessed on Friday 9th September, 2011

[82] [Web/Cogknow.eu] COGKNOW - Project, 2006
http://www.cogknow.eu
Date last accessed on Tuesday 20th September, 2011

[83] [Web/DEStatis.de] DEStatis.de: Hohe Kosten durch Demenz und Depressionen
http://www.destatis.de/jetspeed/portal/cms/Sites/destatis/Internet/
DE/Presse/pm/2010/08/PD10__280__23631,templateId=renderPrint.psml
Date last accessed on Saturday 3rd September, 2011

[84] [Web/DW] DW-WORLD.de: Lebenserwartung steigt auf 100 Jahre
http://www.dw-world.de/dw/article/0,,4755697,00.html
Date last accessed on Tuesday 2nd August, 2011

[85] [Web/Focus.de] Focus.de: Demenz: Zeitbombe Altersverwirrung
http://www.focus.de/gesundheit/ratgeber/gehirn/demenz/
altersverwirrung_aid_25699.html
Date last accessed on Thursday 7th July, 2011

[86] [Web/Focus.de B] Focus.de: Alzheimer: Gentechnik aktiviert Eiweiß-Müllabfuhr
http://www.focus.de/gesundheit/ratgeber/gehirn/news/
alzheimer-gentechnik-aktiviert-eiweiss-muellabfuhr_aid_605597.html
Date last accessed on Saturday 23rd April, 2011

[87] [Web/GMaps] Google Maps: Über Google Maps
http://maps.google.com/support/bin/answer.py?answer=7060
Date last accessed on Sunday 30th October, 2011

[88] [Web/GoGo] GPS: Segments
http://www.100gogo.com/ever1.htm
Date last accessed on Saturday 22nd October, 2011

[89] [Web/iPhoneWiki] iPhoneWiki: Welcome to the iPhone Wiki
http://www.theiphonewiki.com
Date last accessed on Friday 30th September, 2011

[90] [Web/iLBC] iLBC: What is iLBC?
http://ilbcfreeware.org/
Date last accessed on Friday 30th September, 2011

[91] [Web/H.323 vs. SIP] H.323 vs. SIP: Vergleich H.323 und SIP
http://www.voip-information.de/sip-h323/sip-h323.php
Date last accessed on Saturday 31st September, 2011

[92] [Web/HI-Tech] Hi-Tech in Action
http://hitechinaction.blogspot.com/
Date last accessed on Friday 30th September, 2011

[93] [Web/El. Kompendium] SIP-Provider
http://www.elektronik-kompendium.de/sites/kom/1102011.htm
Date last accessed on Friday 30th September, 2011

[94] [Web/UIUC] Head Mounted Display
https://segue.atlas.uiuc.edu/index.php?action=site&site=aangell&
section=5206&page=17228
Date last accessed on Saturday 22nd October, 2011

[95] [Web/SIP Center] What Is SIP Introduction
http://www.sipcenter.com
Date last accessed on Friday 30th September, 2011

[96] [Web/WAAS] faa.gov: GNSS Frequently Asked Questions - WAAS
http://www.faa.gov/about/office_org/headquarters_offices/ato/service_
units/techops/navservices/gnss/faq/waas/
Date last accessed on Wednesday 5th October, 2011

[97] [Web/WKO] WKO.at: Lebenserwartung in Europa
http://www.wko.at/statistik/eu/europa-lebenserwartung.pdf
Date last accessed on Tuesday 2nd August, 2011

A. Interview guide (German)

Allgemeine Angaben

- Zur Person

- Bitte skizzieren Sie kurz den Verlauf der Erkrankung (wann aufgetreten, wesentliche Ereignisse, größte Herausforderungen)

Umwelt/ sich außerhalb des Hauses befinden

- Bekommen Sie professionelle Unterstützung/ Ehrenamtliche Unterstützung?

- Wie organisieren Sie Unterstützung innerhalb der Familie?

- Wie organisieren Sie Aufenthalte außerhalb des Hauses?

- Verbringen Sie viel Zeit außerhalb des Hauses? Wo, mit wem?

- Möchten Sie uns von einer Situation erzählen, wo sie draußen waren und Schwierigkeiten mit der Orientierung hatten?

- Mit welchen Strategien schaffen sie es, mit Orientierungsproblemen zurecht zu kommen, wenn sie alleine unterwegs sind (z.B. Zettel mit Ziel des Spaziergangs mitnehmen, eigene Adresse auf Zettel aufschreiben, Handy)

Alltag im Haus

- Wie sieht ein typischer Tagesablauf aus?

- Was sind die größten Schwierigkeiten?

Technische Hilfen

- Wie schätzen Sie den Nutzen einer technischen Hilfe (wie z.B. ein Help-Yourself Navigationssystem) ein? (die Idee wird im Gespräch genau und verständlich erläutert)

- Was wären aus Ihrer Sicht Problemaspekte in der praktischen Nutzung (kein PC zu Hause, Keine Erfahrung mit Smartphone, etc.)

Im Anschluss zeigen wir ein Programm auf dem Handy und möchten Ihre persönlichen Gedanken und Meinungen dazu sammeln

B. Interview transcript A (German)

Interview mit dem Demenzkranken und dessen Betreuer

I - Interviewer
DI - Dementer Interviewpartner
BI - Betreuender Interviewpartner

Köln, den 01.06.2011

Interviewtranskript

00:02:50 I: *Wie alt sind Sie?*

00:02:51 DI: *47.*

00:02:55 I: *Wann haben Sie erstmals bemerkt, dass Sie Demenz haben?*

00:03:02 DI: *Das war seit des August letztes Jahr diagnostiziert, aber ich habe das wahrscheinlich schon seitlange gehabt.*

00:03:12 I: *Aus welchem Grund haben Sie sich untersuchen lassen?*

00:03:15 DI: *Ich wurde sehr vergesslich und unruhig und man hat mir erzählt, dass es Depression ist. Ich habe immer behauptet, dass es nicht sein kann. Und der Arzt hat festgestellt, dass es doch nicht Depression ist sondern was Anderes.*

00:03:40 I: *Was war die größte Herausforderung?*

00:03:45 DI: *Immer wieder, wenn ich Spaziergänge mit meinem Hund mache, oder, aber es ist mir von Arbeit passiert, ich steige in den Zug und fahre in falsche Richtung oder ich weiß nicht, wo ich bin und mein Hund muss mir helfen, den Weg zurück zu finden. Und wenn es das nicht kann ich nehme das Handy und rufe meine Frau an, sie kommt mich dann abholen.*

00:04:57 I: *Bekommen Sie professionelle Unterstützung?*

00:05:17 DI: *Meine Frau hilft mir.*

00:05:21 BI: *Ich bin Krankenschwester von daher machen wir im Moment alles noch so.*

00:05:30 I: **Wie organisieren Sie Ihr Aufenthalt außerhalb des Hauses Machen Sie Notizen wenn sie nach draußen gehen?**

00:05:45 DI: *Viele Telefonate. Meine Frau ruft mich immer wieder auf der Arbeit an, und denkt da dran welcher Zug ich nehmen soll, in welche Richtung.*

00:05:55 BI: *Bist du jetzt im Zug, bist du losgefahren, bist du bei der Physiotherapie angekommen. Es aber auch anstrengend, wenn man selber arbeitet, weil ich habe meinen eigenen Kopf und meinen eigenen Ablauf und muss, halt, immer gucken auf Uhr gucken, ist er jetzt bei Physiotherapie, oder, er muss jetzt eigentlich in der Bahn sitzen, er muss jetzt eigentlich losgefahren sein. Und da wir solche Situationen haben, wo wir letztens total im verkehrten Zug und verkehrter Richtung saß, „Oh glaube ich in Richtung Essen gefahren". Also, total in verkehrte Stadt , in ganz andere Richtung...*

00:07:40 I: **Verbringen Sie viel Zeit außerhalb des Hauses?**

00:07:45 BI: *Er geht arbeiten.*

00:08:07 I: **Haben Sie immer Schwierigkeiten den Weg zurückzufinden?**

00:08:12 DI: *Ich habe gemerkt, dass einen Weg mehrmals gefahren bin, dann ist es kein Problem, aber wenn gehe ich irgendwo fremdes hin, wo ich mich nicht auskenne, dann habe ich große Probleme.*

00:08:30 BI: *Im diesen Teil da muss auf jeden Fall, irgendwie (dass ist auch ein Zeitproblem), das muss einen Wecker drin sein. Das ist auch ein Weg Problem, aber es ist auch ein Zeitproblem - immer zur richtigen Zeit am richtigen Ort zu sein. Es ist morgens, ist es ganz schwierig da bin ich aber da, bin irgendwie rechtzeitig aus dem Haus am Bus irgendwie hinzukriegen, das ist aber recht schwierig nachmittags rechtzeitig, wenn ich nicht da bin, du muss jetzt losgehen damit du rechtzeitig in der Bahn bist, damit du rechtzeitig bei der Physiotherapie bist. Und das haben wir jeden Tag. Irgendwie muss man das gemanagt kriegen.*

00:09:30 I: **Soll dieses App soll nicht nur den Weg zeigen aber auch als ein Reminder?**

00:09:45 BI: *Wie so ein Manager, Bimmelton - „Jetzt losgehen", wie ein Wecker.*

00:10:00 DI: *Aber, Sie reden von einem App und ich denke, dass es für einen iPhone sein wird, aber ich habe so ein Handy gehabt und konnte mit diesem Display überhaupt nicht klar kommen, weil man drückt nur auf dem Glas und ich schaffte es nicht, ich muss ein Knopf haben.*

00:10:40 I: **Welche Handy haben Sie jetzt?**

00:10:53 BI: *Wir haben ganz altes wieder, weil er das überhaupt nicht geschafft hat, mit den Tasten, weil er brauch diese dicken Tasten.*

00:11:01 DI: *Ich muss einen Gefühl haben dass ich etwas gedrückt habe. Nur auf dem Glas hat mir nicht geholfen.*

00:11:10 BI: *Das ging überhaupt nicht weil er etwas immer weggedrückt hat, Gespräch nicht angenommen.*

00:11:49 I: **Es gibt auch Handys mit großen Display und mit Tasten.**

00:11:52 BI: *Also, er hat kein Alzheimer nur eine klein Hirnatrophie. Das Problem ist ja wenn man dement ist, dass die Koordination der Hände wird auch schlechter, und dass heißt, dass er immer gucken muss, wie er die Sachen überhaupt hält oder drückt und das wird, halt, immer schwieriger werden und da muss man gucken, wie kriegt man das hin, dass derjenige dann noch, das drücken kann überhaupt.*

00:12:30 DI: *Das große Problem ist, dass ich durch so ein Glass nicht bedienen kann.*

00:13:10 I: **Wir machen es für iPhone, aber später, kann sein dass es dafür ein spezielles Gerät geben wird. Das App wird nur wenige(eine „Hilfe") Tasten haben und wir versuchen das App einfach wie möglich zu machen.**

00:14:30 BI: *Das muss was für kranken Leute sein. Am besten einen großen roten Knopf.*

00:15:30 I: **Wie sieht Ihr Tagesablauf aus?**

00:15:40 DI: *Ich gehe arbeiten und ich komme nach Hause...*

00:15:57 BI: *Nein, nach der Arbeit hast du immer - entweder Ergotherapie oder Physiotherapie, ja. Du hast Termine, wo du nach der Arbeit hin musst. Mindestens 3-4 mal in der Woche. Du muss nach der Arbeit immer gucken, dass du pünktlich woanders bist - das mach die Sache schwierig. Das ist die größte Schwierigkeit - pünktlich woanders zu sein.*

00:16:30 I: **Wie schätzen Sie überhaupt die Nutzung von technischer Hilfe? Würden sie so ein System nutzen?**

00:16:45 DI: *Ich werde es benutzen, wenn ich denke, dass wenn ich den Knopf drücke, dann es hilft mir, dass muss nicht so kompliziert sein nicht für einen Techniker.*

00:17:30 BI: *Wichtig glaube ich ist es noch, weil im meisten Situationen, wo es dunkel ist, wenn man so ein Handy aus der Tasche zieht und es ist erstmals dunkel - wichtig ist das diese Hilfe-Knopf leuchtet, weil die Situationen, wo er gestanden hat und nicht mehr nach Hause gefunden hat, das war immer draußen im Dunkeln und ich glaube wenn er Handy aus der Tasche zieht soll dieser Knopf leuchten, wissen Sie „Aha, roter Knopf - drücken".*

00:20:00 I: **Dann wurde das Konzept der Anwendung erklärt.**

00:21:10 DI: *Finde es gut, dass ich meiner Frau nicht erklären muss, wo ich mich befinde.*

00:21:20 BI: *Letztes mal du sagtest, dass du auf dem Bank bist, aber du wars nicht auf dem Bank.*

00:23:10 I: **Für die Betreuung braucht man einen PC mit Internetverbindung. Haben Sie die Möglichkeit zu Hause oder auf der Arbeit Ihrem Mann zu betreuen?**

00:23:40 BI: *Zu Hause - Ja, auf der Arbeit nein, weil ich immer unterwegs bin.*

00:23:45 I: **Welches Handy haben Sie?**

00:23:50 BI: *Auch ein altes Handy.*

00:25:05 I: **Wenn Sie Schwierigkeiten haben den Weg wieder zurückzufinden, was ist Ihre erste Gedanke? Versuchen Sie zu erst selber den Weg zu finden oder suchen Sie sofort Hilfe?**

00:26:17 DI: *Genau, teilweise mein Hund hilft mir dabei.*

00:26:25 BI: *Aber letztes Mal stand er neben dir auf dem Feld. Also die Beiden haben nichts gemacht bis ich kommen bin.*

00:26:50 I: **Wie haben Sie damals ihm gefunden?**

00:27:00 BI: *Wir sagen ihm immer, er soll sein Handy mitnehmen. Ich habe auf Uhr geguckt und als er nicht wiederkam, dann habe ich ihn angerufen und sagte wo bist du - „Weiß auch nicht" - das ist nicht gut... „Ich glaube auf einer Bank" - Ich wusste ungefähr die Richtung, und bin ich in die ungefähre Richtung gegangen, habe ich ihn dahinten irgendwo stehen. Was mein Leben leicht machen kann ist der Supermarkt, weil er immer wegrennt, er rennt immer irgendwohin und wir brauchen immer mindestens 5 Telefonate, bis wir ihn wieder haben, weil er weg ist.*

00:30:30 I: **Detaillierte Erklärung von Anwendung.**
Wie finden Sie es?

00:30:57 DI: *Es ist sehr nützlich, damit könnte mich mit so einem Teil orientieren.*

00:34:57 I: **Gedächtnismerkmale, wie finden Sie es?**

00:35:17 DI: *Gut.*

00:37:35 BI: *Wir haben verschiedene Merkmale mit ihm... Du bist schon müde?*

00:37:58 DI: *Ja ich bin schon müde.*

00:36:37 BI: *Ich glaube noch dass es bei Menschen mit Demenz wichtig ist - Immer das Gleiche - Immer der gleiche Ablauf - Immer das Gleiche, das Gleiche, das Gleiche! Was wir noch auf der Arbeit gemerkt, er kann im Grunde genommen nur die Sachen, die er noch aus Altgedächtnis kann, aber als er was neues aus neuem Computer Programm lernen sollte - ging überhaupt nicht.*

00:37:26 DI: *Was ich vor 14 Jahren gelernt habe - das kann ich, aber was Neues - ich komme damit nicht klar.*

00:38:00 I: **Wie finden Sie es, wenn ein Plan von Ihnen vorher gemacht?...**

00:38:35 BI: *Das Problem ist ja ich praktisch daran denken muss, und die Frage ist, gibt es irgendwelche Möglichkeit, das irgendwie zu entspannen zu entlasten, weil die Situation gehen dann schief, wenn ich genau zu den Zeitpunkt einen Termin habe, sei es bei der Bank oder Patienten, wenn ich ihn eigentlich anrufen musste, um ihm zu sagen - jetzt muss du in die S-Bahn einsteigen. In dem Moment musste eigentlich irgendwie bimmeln, und sagen „Jetzt muss du in die Bahn einsteigen". Ja, aber das nutzt nichts, wenn ich morgens ihm ein Zettel gebe, wo alles da steht - das bringt Garnichts, das haben wir schon probiert. Es muss eine akustische Meldung kommen.*

C. Interview transcript B (German)

Interview mit Betreuer des Demenzkranken

I - Interviewer
DI - Dementer Interviewpartner
BI - Betreuender Interviewpartner

Kreuztal, den 14.06.2011

Interviewtranskript

00:02:55-7 I: *Wie alt Sind Sie und ihre Mutter?*

00:03:07-9 BI: *Ich 48, meine Mutter 86.*

00:03:16-0 I: *Sie Leben mit ihre Mutter zusammen*

00:03:18-4 BI: *Ja seit einem halben Jahr. Meine Mutter leidet an Demenz, ein Demenz ist ein rissen Wort, ne, also hat ganz viele Fassaden und meine Mutter gehört zu denjenigen, bei der man das nicht merken würde, wenn man das nicht wüsste, weil ganz elegante Fassaden haben. Sie würde jetzt hier sitzen und sich freuen, „hahah" und „ja" und... - gut, das ist eine Seite. Erkennt man so eine Demenz... in der man täglichen Umgang miteinander immer lernt, dass die Antworten sind Floskeln - die passen zwar immer, die sind für außenstehenden völlig sofort an richtiger Stelle, da weißt Insider wie ich, dass die Verbindung nicht macht. Und das dauert für allen Beteiligten auch für mich in gewissen Verantwortlichkeit stecken, dass man für sich selber ein Schlussstrich ziehen muss, sagen wie ist es jetzt, sonst fängt man nämlich an - „stimmt das jetzt?" - und das ist jetzt nicht so und dass Sie jetzt Schild um hat, das finde ich ganz entscheidend jetzt im Moment ist meine Antwort in einer dementen Fase. Man reagiert oft da oft ungerecht andererseits sind die Situationen da denkt - man das gibt's nicht. Und dann kommt diese Mutter-Tochter... das gibt's bei jeder Generation, das ist aber ein anderes Thema, aber das ist ganz entscheidend... Schwierig ist die rollen tausch. Für meine Mutter ist es schwierig, dass Sie durchaus in der Lage ist erkennen, wenn sie die Sache nicht nachvollziehen kann* und dann kommen solche Erklärungsmuster, wie... also dann man hat andere.. *Sie erkennt das und schiebt diesen Mangel an Andere ab.*

00:06:29-9 I: **Wie erklären Sie das, dass ist es Scham**

00:06:34-1 BI: *Ja, oder auch dass man sich selber nicht eingestehen will. Also, bringen sich selben in die Situation, das ist ganz schwierig. Und manchmal kommt auch, also meine Mutter ist jetzt nicht aggressiv, aber die kriegen dann eure schlechte Laune, wie wir alle das auch kriegen, wenn man mit etwas unzufrieden ist. Und fängt der Kreislauf an mit Überforderung, dann kommt gewisse körperliche Eingeschränktheit hinzu, und also Demenz geht immer mit dem Körper mit. Also das weiß ich mittlerweile. Gibt es im Kopf Schwäche, dann... und man wird unbeweglicher - wie im Kopf so auch im Geist.*

00:07:33-4 I: **Sie sagten jetzt grade dass Sie seit einem halben Jahr mit ihrer Mutter zusammenleben. Ist es dann so, dass vor einem halben Jahr, gab es ein Wandel in der Erkrankung**

00:07:46-1 BI: *Also diese Wandel kommt ganz schleichend, den sieht man erst immer Nachhinein, und ich gehe ja mit betriebsblind. Wir haben Zweifamilienhaus. Jetzt kommt für mich die Situation hinzu, dass mein Ehemann vor ein paar Jahren gestorben ist. Meine Mutter hat unten gelebt, und dann habe ich für mich Dinge entschieden, weile meine Mutter unten überfordert war - das ist eine 80 m2 Wohnung. Sie sucht permanent die Dinge, oder man muss den Kühlschrank beaufsichtigen und, und... und ich habe meinem Sohn und seiner festen Freundin unten diese Wohnung angeboten, und im Tausch wohnt meine Mutter im Prinzip in meiner Wohnung - 2 Zimmer. Wenn das Verhältnis zwischen meiner Mutter und mir im Grundsatz nicht stimmen würde oder immer gestimmt hätte, also da gibt es natürlich diese üblichen Animositäten, ich hätte das überhaupt nicht gemacht. Und bin ich jetzt selber bisschen erwischt, jetzt erschlägt es mich manchmal. Und seit halben Jahr, das ungefähr dieser Zeit, erkrankt und sich verschlimmert hat. Und jetzt dieser Ortswechsel, bringt ganz viele Aufhängepunkte, wo sie jetzt Dinge wieder vermisst, die sie mir wieder ankreiden kann - ankreiden - weil sie es nicht finden. Andererseits es ist auch sehr großzügig von ihr, ich habe es ihr erklärt, aus dem und dem Grund... ich habe noch einem jungen Sohn... sie hat ganz alles total akzeptiert und gibt das ihrem Enkel und mir, also aus ganz lieben... - ganz super eigentlich, aber zusammenleben hier erfordert ganz viel, und im Moment bin ich diejenige die zahlt - gesundheitlich, nervlich... das ist nicht immer eins, das ist ja klar. Das ist die Situation.*

00:10:25-8 I: **Deswegen haben Sie den Schritt gemacht bei der „Auszeit"...?**

00:10:31-2 BI: *Das geht schon seit einem Jahr und noch länger wahrscheinlich, dass ich einfach nicht mehr in der Pflicht bin... Also z.B. beim Kuchen, ich denke ja mach doch, und dann sieht die Küche aus wie Sau und es ist meine Zeit alles wieder... - das ist Handlungsabbrüche... Oder, sie raucht, „Ich habe keine Zigaretten ich muss nach Fischars" - ich sage - du gehst nicht alleine. Und sie hat das im Kopf das sie es schafft, aber sie schafft es nicht - total fertig... sie kommt wieder zurück wir sind ja auf dem Dorf jeder erkennt sie... Sie kommt nach Hause, das ist überhaupt kein Problem. Und ich habe das auch erlebt das sie rausgeschlichen ist und es ist auf ein mal Treppen - überhaupt kein Hindernis - wenn ich da bin - „ach die Treppe..." Meine Mutter ist manchmal sehr orientierungslos - das ist aber Fasen - und dann ist es ihr alles klar und sie ist sehr sehr wacklig - ich denke meine Mutter ist in einem*

Stadium ist dass Sie immer nach Hause finden würde, sondern dass sie aufgrund ihrer Körperlichkeit, dann nicht mehr könnte. ... Aber das sie es vorher nicht einschätzen können, also sie nehmen ganz viel vor und man glaubt das, und letztlich macht sie doch Rückzug.

00:13:16-0 I: *Die Autonomie Problematik. Sie haben gerade erwähnt Rollentausch, sie wollen wahrscheinlich das nicht...*

00:13:36-6 BI: *Beide möchten das nicht. Ich möchte im Prinzip auch zu meiner Mutter kommen alles so von die Füße ... wie man das als Kind gemacht, aber das alles ist schon durch.*

00:13:51-2 I: *Könnte Sie da noch was zu sagen, wie da so Ihre Strategien sind? Sie habe schon paar mal gesagt, dass sie dann sagen „Mach doch"...*

00:14:01-4 BI: *Das ist meine Wut. Wut, „gehe bitte...", „wenn du..." und dann erwische ich sie an klaren Momenten und das sagt sie mir „da ist es doch eine Ampel...", „da ist es doch eine Bürgersteig..." Ich versuche diese Gefahren , die ich sehe zu erklären, ich sehe mich immer in Erklärungsbedarf, das kann ich mir auch sparen, das kommt nicht an, weil sie es auch dann nicht sehen will. Da ist sie ganz Mensch, das tuen wir auch gerne - wir holen uns immer die Erklärungsversuche, die wir brauchen und passen. Das alles ist nachvollziehbar, aber Aufgrund von , kann ich auch nicht beurteilen... Habe ich kein gutes Gefühl... Das kann ich jetzt gar nicht genau sagen*

00:15:38-2 I: *Wurde das diagnostiziert?*

00:15:40-1 BI: *2007 aber da sind es Nachhinein Signale oder Situationen gewesen, die schon früher drauf hingedeutet haben. Das erkennt man aber rückblickend, wenn man sich da dran erinnert.*

00:16:11-0 I: *Bekommt Sie professionelle Unterstützung?*

00:16:25-6 BI: *Vor einem Monat geht Sie zu einer Tagespflege, wird abgeholt und gebracht. Sie sagt den Anderen, dass ihr super gut geht, das stimmt auch. Das ist eine Entscheidung, die aus meinem Egoismus erwächst. Und meine ist so genugsam. Ist sehr erschöpft, wenn sie wieder kommt. Sie geht 2 mal die Woche. Von Morgens bis Nachmittags, von 8 bis 16 Uhr. In Hilchenbach.*

00:17:54-8 I: *Wie organisieren sie Unterstützung innerhalb Familie?*

00:18:09-8 BI: *Ich halte mich so gut ich es kann aus allem was man meiner Mutter so an Programm bittet raus. Also ich habe noch eine Schwester, die 2 mal die Woche kommt und mindestens Sonntags mit ihr Kaffee trinken fährt. Und jetzt weiß ich das in der Tagespflege sie auch spazieren gehen und und und... Aber nach wie vor ist meiner Mutter, dadurch dass sie so hier lebt hat unglaublich viel Programm, alles sie kriegt alles mit. Kaffee trinken, sie fährt durch die Gegend fahren.*

00:19:33-0 I: *Alleine geht sie nicht spazieren?*

00:19:35-4 BI: *Nein. Sie käme nicht auf die Idee, sie hat zwar, also wir kommen aus ziemlich sportlicher Familie, sie muss sich ja bewegen, aber, sie würde niemals alleine gehen, sie sagt nur wenn sie einkaufen will, das ist die Rolle die Ihr fehlt, dann geht sie und das schadet mir auch nichts, vielleicht kommt so eine Argumentation raus, die sie mir gegenüber hat, das kann ich nicht beurteilen, muss ich das rechtfertigen, über die Bewegung.*

00:20:26-0 I: **Das Ort, wohin sie Einkaufen geht ist wahrscheinlich nicht weit entfernt von hier?**

00:20:30-0 BI: *Sie tut es nicht, und wenn nur im Begleitung...*

00:21:14-1 I: **Wenn Sie so eine Anwendung hätten, würden Sie sie alleine einkaufen gehen lassen?**

00:21:25-4 BI: *Nein. Ich bin bestimmt nicht so medienfit... Ich kann damit umgehen und kann damit über-leben meine Mutter erklären meine Söhne und auch ich das Prinzip eines Computers oder eines Handys, sie kann also auch nicht mit einem Handy umgehen. Konnte sie natürlich, aber sie geht jetzt nicht ans Telefon, sie weiß nicht welcher Knopf ist zu drücken gilt. Würde die überfordern. Es seiden,.. es kommt mir die Gedanke, meine Mutter hat die Pflegestufe 2 und sie ist mal gestürzt und dann hat eine befreundete Krankenschwester gesagt, wir bestellen alles so es gibt, Rollstuhl, Toilettenstuhl... egal vielleicht brauch sie es im Moment und kommt alles wieder weg, aber es ist da und sie sieht es und die Begegnung ist nicht neue das ist schon ganze Zeitlang im Prinzip damit leben kann aber jetzt, glaube ich, in so einer dementen Fase so ein neues Teil, könnte man es sparen... Geht überhaupt nicht... Da ist überhaupt keinen Gedanken dann.. für die das bedienen lies... jetzt will ich nicht vorgreifen in Ihrer Entwicklung, wie einfach das wäre oder oder...*

00:23:25-4 I: **Sie sagten das Sie Ihre Mutter nicht alleine spazieren gehen lassen würden. Können Sie sagen warum?**

00:23:44-7 BI: *Körperliche und gewisse Orientierungslosigkeit, wobei nicht so weit geht, dass sie überhaupt nicht mehr weiß, wo sie ist, zumindest im Moment nicht. Aber ich beobachte, wenn sie auf der Straße steht, dass sie guckt, wo muss ich jetzt denn hin.*

00:24:10-3 I: **Aber Ihre Mutter also bewegt sich von selbst nicht weit vom Haus weg**

00:24:15-5 BI: *Nein.*

00:24:20-8 I: **Hat sie Alzheimer?**

00:24:24-3 BI: *Nein, Sie hat eine Demenz...*

00:24:39-3 I: **Sie haben gesagt sie ist 2 mal der Woche Tagespflege hat es mit Auszeit zu tun?**

00:24:54-8 BI: *Nein die sind voneinander unabhängig*

00:25:00-0 I: **Und da kommen auch Leute hierhin?**

00:25:02-2 BI: *Ja da ist es eine Dame gekommen, sie kommt auch aus dem Dorf und die geht mit sie spazieren, wenn Wetter es zulässt, nimmt sie mit und gehen sie anderswo spazieren.*

00:25:21-0 I: **Haben Sie da ein festen Termin?**

00:25:23-0 BI: *Ja*

00:25:28-4 I: **Wie sieht ein typischer Tagesablauf aus?**

00:25:33-0 BI: *Meine Mutter gehört zu denjenigen, die ganz lange schlaffen können, was ich gut finde, normal ist um 10Uhr aufstehen, sie sitzt abends lange vor Fernseher. Wir sind beide nicht für Morgen geboren und dann habe ich schlechte Fase hinter mir. Dann steht sie auf, das dauert bei meiner Mutter, das dauert alles unglaublich. Sie sitzt gerne im Morgenmantel. Die Küche ist immer ein Bezugspunkt, weil sie immer in Küche gelebt. Sie wissen was ich meine... Dann kommt das Waschen. Das unglaublich dauert ich helfe ihr, unterstütze sie, was auch ein Problem ist für sie. Ich werde immer etwas ungeduldig. Dan muss sie unbedingt essen - würde sie verhungern. Dann zieht sie sich bisschen zurück oder geht und ihre Wohnzimmer oder nestelt an ihrem Bett herum. Meine Mutter hat immer feste Mahlzeiten. Ich habe es nicht immer rechtzeitig geschafft, weil bei mir hier 120 Leute rein und raus kommen, und ich hatte Putzhilfe und dann kommt dies Frau von Auszeit und die sind immer in meine Wohnung. Ich habe überhaupt keine Geheimnisse, aber das war auf einmal viel. Ich bin auch berufstätig und dann habe ich das alles wieder abgeblasen, warum habe ich das alles gesagt und genau dieses Kochen. Kochen ist nicht mein Ding ich betrachte es als eine Notwendigkeit das ist auch ein Reibungspunkt auch zwischen meiner Mutter und mir, aber ich versuche das immer hinzukriegen, weil ich nachmittags arbeite. Ich arbeite als Englischdozentin in verschiedenen Bildungseinrichtungen. Für mich geht Mittags dieser Alarm los, mein Sohn kommt nach Hause dann kommt nächster Streitpunkt - meine Mutter will spülen und ich bin nur daran interessiert das sie es nicht tut, weil es nicht sauber ist, sie kriegt es nicht sauber genug. Ich bin nicht pingelig aber das ist ein Dauerzustand, der immer wieder kommt. Mein junger Sohn kommt aus der Schule. Dann zieht meine Mutter zurück und strickt, Strümpfe, sie hat lebenslang gerne gestrickt, aber sie stellt höhe Ansprüche, für zwei Strümpfe braucht sie unglaublich lange, nicht die Fase des Strickens, bis das fertig ist, sondern sie zieht es nur auf. Das ist ihre Aufgabe das ist ihr Ding. Sie zieht das immer wider auf, sie scheitert aber an ihrer eigenen Anspruch, wie wir alle das tun - aber ich sage es ihnen das ist alles mit meine Brille. Um 8 guck sie Fernseher Nachrichten und das was dahinter kommt egal - dann muss diese ding lauten. Das finde ich das gut.*

00:33:42-4 I: **Wie ist es, wenn sie das macht, haben sie das Gefühl dass es tut ihr nicht gut?**

00:33:53-5 BI: *Das ist ihr völlig egal, also, was heißt egal sie wird sich ärgern, weil sie das sieht.*

00:34:33-3 I: **Was sind die größten Schwierigkeiten für Ihre Mutter?**

00:35:07-0 BI: *Von der ich denken würde, welche Antwort sie gäbe, wenn Sie sie direkt fragen würden?*

00:35:11-6 I: **Ja.**

00:35:12-2 BI: *Diese Treppe hier. Sich zurechtzufinden in der Küche.*

00:35:41-3 I: **Wäre für Sie auch oder für Ihre Mutter verbunden mit einem Verlust Autonomie.**

00:35:51-5 BI: *Ja das sagt sie. Also sie hat z.B. gesagt, dass „wenn ich hier oben bin, dann hast mich unter deinem ..." hat sie gesagt. ganz klar formuliert.*

00:36:27-7 I: **Was sind die größten Schwierigkeiten für Sie?.**

00:36:32-5 BI: *Die ich für meine Mutter formulieren würde oder meine?*

00:36:36-3 I: *Ihre eigene die Sie selber formulieren... den es ist interessant das es sich 3 Sichten entwerfen - was hat Ihre Mutter direkt, was sehen Sie als Problem Ihrer Mutter - sagen sie doch bitte das erstmals*

00:36:54-5 BI: *Ich denke, dass es für meine Mutter schwierig ist diese Rolle abzugeben, diese Mutter Rolle, und ihre Schwäche zu erkennen und zu akzeptieren und dass sie auf Hilfe ihrer Tochter in manchen Dingen angewiesen ist, wo es ihr angenehm ist, aber andererseits sieht sie es ganz gerne. Sie hat sehr viel abgegeben. Und ich für mich formuliere da reicht wirklich nicht Zeit, sie erwischen mich, wo ich ganz hart dran arbeite. Weniger arbeiten einfach, damit hier wieder Ruhe einkehrt. Ich habe gute Laune hat ganze Haus gute Laune. Ich habe im Moment Neurodermitis Attacke. Ich bin Buchstäblich angekratzt. Natürlich ist meine Situation besonders, aber dadurch, dass alleine lebe... kein Schwiegersohn wird man glaube ich keinem zumuten... Es ist mein Haus ich entscheide da und ich komme damit zu recht... manchmal wenn ich merke das meine Mutter kommt, diesen schlurfenden Gang, könnte ich manchmal explodieren, ehrlich gesagt. Sie, dann schon so rücksichtsvoll war, weil wir mehrheitlich in der Küche, und sie wollte mich nicht stören, wenn sie an keinem Brot dran kam, was ich aber dachte dass auch nicht sein kann, das ist genauso schrecklich wie ich... dieses Empfinden - es stört sie. Niemand gezogen mich diese Situation hier zu machen. Andererseits weiß ich auch von anderen, zu meiner Generation ist es das Thema, dieser Spagat nach oben und nach unten. ich hätte sie auch unten wohnen lassen können, dann wäre dieser Abstand da gewesen, nur weil man die Tür zu macht, das ist Egoismus für mich gewesen und in sich passt die Situation, so eine Verankerung, eine nimmt von anderen, passt irgendwie, aber letztlich bin nur ich gefragt für mich da die Dinge zu verändern oder Einstellung.*

00:41:37-2 I: *Bekommen Sie auch da professionelle Hilfe?*

00:42:57-5 BI: *Sobald ich Dinge formuliere kriegen sie überhaupt erst Boden das ist hilfreich, aber ansonsten jemand wie meine Mutter, sich darstelle in ihrem Person oder Entwicklung und in ihre Degeneration und die wird alt fertig da wart nicht dieser Aufbau dahinter... und wie alle Dingen seine Berechtigung hat, weil immer mehr Leute immer älter werden, dadurch steigt dieser Anteil... Für mich ist völlig klar das ich jetzt nicht, dass ich in so ein Kreis gehen würde, weil dann drehe ich das erst recht. Ich drehe es hier auch schon, schon wieder, ich will auf keinen Fall verdrängen, aber dann auch hinzugehen und dann es noch mal von anderen anzuhören... das ist... die Nuancen und die Gestalt ist unterschiedlich, aber das Prinzip immer das gleiche. und ich muss zu Ruhe kommen ich muss meine eigenen gedanklichen Kreisen ziehen, man muss mich in Ruhe lassen und ich brauche für alle Dinge, die ich so Angriff nehme, seit es Garten oder Gestalten oder sonst irgendwas, so eine Vorlaufzeit ich brauche für mich alleine... ich fand sehr viel über Bewegung, abbauen, also ich brauche auf jeden Fall so eine Ruhe Fase, so mit einer Entspannungsmusik... Die Lösung habe ich in mir...Das ist gut, wenn man es so auch nach Außen... ich muss so irgendjemandem...*

00:45:55-2 I: *Beschreibung de Systems*

00:53:36-2 BI: *Das kann ich nicht beurteilen, weil ich Angehörigen bin - wie weit das mir Sicherheit gibt - als für meine Mutter wäre das.. - also das könnte ich mir sparen. Ich würde in ihrem Fall überhaupt keinen Sinn dran sehen. Ich aber weiß das man formuliert „dann gehe!" oder nach Motte „dann soll es eben so sein" man ist dazu nicht in der Lage - zeitlich nicht, auffassungstechnisch nicht jemanden so zu überwachen. Es gibt immer so Fasen wo sie alleine ist und wenn es Sie eben in Sinn kommt, dann geht sie eben - dann ist es da so ein Problem - wo kein Richter da kein Kläger - außer meiner Schwester, wer hat da Verantwortlichkeit in wie weiht man das gibt. Und ich denke das so ein System wieder bindet an die Person, sie ist weg, aber man hat immer dauerhaft in Bewusstsein. Bei Demenz ist es nicht die körperlicher Arbeit, ja dafür braucht man messbare Zeit, aber das was man im Kopf hat, was nicht loslässt - das ist das Zermürbend und ich glaube das geht allen so.*

00:56:16-9 I: **Welche Gedanken sind es, die nicht loslassen? Verantwortungsgefühle?**

00:57:00-9 BI: *Sie wissen es ja... wen man etwas plant - Wie ist es das dem Kind zurecht? Was brauche ich alles? Was macht das? Wann? Wie? Wie kommen die von A nach B? und.. und.. und.. Also, wenn man alleine weg will, plant man das alles irgendwie, ist es Mann da? oder Bruder da? ist Oma da? mein junger Sohn ist 14 - das ist überhaupt kein Problem, aber es wiederholen sich genau diese Gedankenmuster... Wenn ich für 2 Tagen zu meinem Verwanden fahre und würde bewusst meine Mutter nicht mitnehmen, ich will bewusst weg, wer ist da? wie kann das gehen? wen muss ich impfen? Wen muss ich anrufen? Hat sie was zu Essen? Kann ich sie so lassen? Das ist immer im Kopf. Dazu erfühlt, dass ich auch manchmal bewusst oder unbewusst Dinge, die mit meiner Mutter überhaupt nicht zu tun haben, darein projizieren. Dann sind wir wieder bei Mutter Tochter Konflikt... Die Animositäten, die man gehabt hat die werden lebenslang, potenzieren sich... und gehe ich noch ein Schritt weiter, dass man das selber in sich hat... die aber darein spielen, über diese Nähe. Es hat keiner dazu gezwungen, ich halte die Entscheidung nach wie vor für richtig, weil es für mich einfacher ist, ich muss mir nicht um 2 Wohnungen kümmern. Ich habe unter meinem Sohn mit seiner Freundin - das klappt alles wunderbar und trotzdem... das ist eine Thema und was dazu kommt, es ist ländlich hier, man unterhält sich, meistens die Frauen die pflegen, die sich um Eltern Schwiegereltern kümmern die schlagen nach dem sie gepflegt haben o der sich endlich entschlossen haben ins Altenheim abzugeben in Weidenau auf, Sie wissen es, was für ein Ort es ist, ne... für psychisch angeschlagene , die bleiben da 6 Wochen, da kann ich Ihnen 6 Personen pflegenden Angehörigen nennen, sie schlagen da drauf, weil sie nicht mehr können. Und ich für mich ich merke dass es losgeht, weil jeder ist dafür empfänglich. Und ich weiß nicht warum es so anstrengt. Das wirklich ein sehr sensibles Thema. Ich könnte es anders drehen, ich könnte auch sagen „Ich darf"...*

01:03:45-8 I: **Was ist über das „Können"?**

01:06:09-9 BI: *Ich beklage mich auch mit Recht, ich gehöre bestimmt nicht zu denjenigen, die so beleidigt sind und ich gelte als stark, aber im Moment das kratzt mich und ich muss... das ist für mich ein 'Challenge'... und das muss ich sehr viel dafür vorbereiten... diese Zeit möchte ich mir gerne geben, die ich mir aber nicht geben kann oder will - ich weiß es nicht genau - weil ich so einen Ratenschwanz im Hinterkopf habe... und ich frage mich brauche ich das, wem muss ich was beweisen? Muss ich nicht... ist es wieder aufgeben? und ich kümmere mich dem, dem ich irgendwie gewachsen bin oder mache ganz konsequenten Schritt und packe meine Mutter - das ist aller letzter Schritt und selbst da ist es nicht vorbei, also wenn sie in Altenheim unter sind, ist es Bewusstsein des schlechten Gewissens, wie sie ist versorgt? und und und... das hörte ich von Leuten die im Altenheimen sind... und trotzdem denke ich, dass diesen Schritt machen werden, würde... Anfang Januar hat sie mir gesagt „Wer man junge Mann der neben dir saß?" das war mein Sohn, ihr Enkel - das war ein mal, aber wenn die Eltern ihre*

Kinder nicht mehr erkennen wie viel Schmerz ist es da für Kinder verbunden... Ich habe keine Ahnung, wie da reagiere...

01:18:25-2 I: **Wenn ich mit Ihre Mutter einen Gespräch führen würde, wie müsste ich dann das aufsetzen? Sieht sie das überhaupt als Krankheit?**

01:18:53-0 BI: *Nein. Sie ist dann bisschen aufgeregt, aber das ist überhaupt kein Problem. Sie denkt sie wurde geprüft in gewisser Weise.*

01:25:33-3 I: **...Macht unser System für Sie nicht viel Sinn...**

01:25:43-2 BI: *Nein, würde überhaupt nicht wissen, wie damit umzugehen... Und jemand der so Lauften-denzen hat, der ist in seiner Krankheit so fortgeschritten, dass der würde ihn ja sagen dann, dass „ich brauch es nicht", „ich brauche keine Hilfe um mich zu orientieren", weil sie, ja, sich sicher sind, wo sie hingehen, das ist so meine Gedanke...*

01:28:56-0 I: **Das kann unterschiedlich sein...**

D. Interview transcript C (German)

Interview mit dem Demenzkranken und dessen Betreuer

I - Interviewer
DI - Dementer Interviewpartner
BI - Betreuender Interviewpartner

Kreuztal, den 14.06.2011

Interviewtranskript

00:03:35-7 BI: *Sie sagt, dass sie keine Hilfe braucht, sie kann noch alles allein. Sie war immer sehr selbsttätig und hat unglaublich viel gemacht und in ihrem Leben viel durchgemacht und jetzt würde sie sich schlecht Helfen lassen aber sie kann aber so vieles nicht und von Zeit zu Zeit wird sie richtig böse, neulich hat sie gesagt sie wäre nicht vergesslich, wir wären vergesslich, gut jetzt ich weiß es ist die Krankheit... manchmal bin ich ganz fix und fertig manchmal geht es nicht mehr. Mein Mann ist im Moment sehr angespannt, der kriegt jetzt 27. Untersuchung und danach entscheidet sich, ob sie Chemo weiter machen oder sie abbrechen. Und da ist er entsprechend nervös und das muss ich alles auffangen und der Sohn auch noch, der macht 2. Studium an der Uni, der hat Architektur abgeschlossen und nicht bekam... war zwischenzeitlich in Australien, jetzt macht er sozial Arbeit, muss aber zwischen durch arbeiten und geht es deswegen nicht voran, macht paar Stunden was... Sie kocht morgens oder ich helfe ihr dabei, früher hat sie sehr gut gekocht. Ich soll nicht immer für sie mitkochen, da sagt sie nein, da „muss ich mein Kopf gar nicht anstrengen" aber was sie jetzt kocht ist manchmal... sie hat fantastisch gekocht, weinachten für ganze Familie und gebacken, aber jetzt dauert es so lange... und ich muss jetzt gucken ob es sie rechtzeitig aus dem Herd holt, sie sagt es auch das es nicht so sein soll als ich sie kontrolliere, ich sage „ich wollte nur gucken wie weit bist du denn.." Ich lehre viel... meine Schwiegermutter war auch Dement...*

00:07:10-1 I: **Wie kommt es Sie andere Haltung haben?**

90

00:07:17-1 BI: *Ich bin lange Jahre ehrenamtlich in VDK(Sozialverband) im Vorstand und da haben wir Seminare. Sollten Sie eigentlich kennen, den sollten Sie bei älteren Leuten weiterempfehlen. Die gehen wen jemand z.B. einer seine Rente nicht durchkriegt, die gehen vor Gericht, die streiten jedes Jahr einige Millionen für die Leute, die ein Rollstuhl brauchen oder irgendwelche Hilfsmittel und die Kasse lehnt das ab, die gehen dahin, die haben eine Lobby. Da wird einiges gemacht. Ich war 16 ehrenamtlich in Vorstand, da war eine Frau , die hat so Seminare gemacht und dann erklärt. Gut jetzt ist es hier im Haus, meine Schwiegermutter wurde nicht im Haus, ich will im Haus keinen Streit also es ist auch passiert, dass ich hochgegangen bin und... denn paar Tage bin ich nicht untergegangen, weil sie kann über Tage bocken da braucht sie nicht reden, dann ist sie so stur... ja, meine Tochter ist in Wiesbaden, die sagt Mutti dann musst du halt drüber wegsehen und ich sage du bist weit genug weg... und mein Sohn er ist in Siegen, der hat an der Uni zu tun, der muss neben aber arbeiten... er kommt auch kurz „Oma geht dir gut?..", „ich fahr mal mit dir"... wir machen auch viel mit ihr wir packen ins Auto und machen eine Fahrt und zum Kaffe über Wochenende immer mit ihr Kaffe trinken, essen, wir kümmern viel um sie, aber manchmal braucht man einfach Ruhe. Jetzt kommt 2 mal der Woche eine Frau aus Auszeit, die spielt dann mit ihr, 2 Stunden... „Mensch ärger dich nicht" und schaut sich die ganzen alten Alpen an, die wir schon gesehen haben bis zum Abwinken... und am Wochenende kommen die Enkelkinder, meine Tochter bringt die Kinder und wollen mal paar im Köln, wir paar Nächte durchschlafen... Mein Mann spielt mit seinen Enkelkinder, aber er darf nicht rennen, weil er hat in Knochen...*

00:11:17-3 I: **Seit wann ist es bei Ihrer Mutter? Welche Veränderung haben Sie gemerkt?**

00:11:21-5 BI: *Wir haben es seit 2 Jahren gemerkt. Sie hat immer den Garten gemacht. Wir haben ihr freies Hand gelassen im Garten und dann merkte ich, dass sie es nicht mehr kann und ich habe gesagt: machen wir das zusammen, ich habe gesät sie hat da gehabt. Dann hat sie gesagt „ich lege die Bohren" sage ich „Gut", „Schaffst du das noch?" „ja!"... dann sagt sie die Boden kommen dies Jahr gar nicht und dann haben wir bemerkt sie verräumte alles, ich sage uns jeder Tag ist Ostern - wir suchen alles, dann schreibt sie meinem Mann einen Zettel, ich brauche dringend 2 Päckchen Puderzucker, ich guck nach - sie hat noch 6 Päckchen. Wir haben das erst im Garten merkten, das sie da Unsinn macht und dann eben ich sag „...die hat heute Geburtstag" sie sagt „nein, die hat erst nächsten Monat", dann überbrückt sie das „Ach so, ich dachte wir hätten jetzt schon... „. Oder wenn sie irgendwas falsch gemacht hat oder sie hat ihre Tabletten nicht genommen „Ach ja das wollte ich jetzt gerade...", da haben wir da auch gemerkt sie nam falsch Tabletten oder doppelt sie hat dann mal abends drei Adompran genommen, dann konnte sie nicht schlaffen, das hat öfter schon mal.., und wir bestellen die Tabletten und gehen immer runter und gucken so, ob die raus sind, weil wenn wir sagen hast du die genommen, das geht nicht. Man muss immer ganz vorsichtig, weil sie immer eine Frau war, die immer ziemlich dominant war. Sie war erst mit 25 Witwe und Vertreibung mit kleinem Kind und ihrer alten Mutter und dann hat sie Mann mit 3 Kindern, Witwer mit 3 Kinder geheiratet. Sie hat sehr viel leisten müssen und ist dementsprechend - sie will das bestimmen. Und dann muss ich halt jetzt vorsichtig sein... jetzt sage ich „du brauchst neuen Mantel", „Ich brauche doch kein Mantel", ich sage „wir gehen mal gucken"... Sobald sie hat das Gefühl, dass wir bestimmen „Ich lass von euch nichts bestimmen"... Und Urenkel ist auch aufgewachsen - sie weiß gar nicht wie alt die sind, das hat früher nicht vorgekommen. Wir merken das es auch auf die Kräften auswirkt, sie kann sehr schlecht laufen, sie geht mit Rollator, aber mitten auf der Straßen. Und dann es gab hier Kaninchen in dem Park und da ging sie jeden Tag und* machte so einen Sack Futter für die. Da haben wir auch da sagt „das stimmt doch nicht mehr mit ihr".. Und jetzt ist es auch so, ich meine, die Gummistrümpfe, ist klar, die ziehe ich an und aus, und ich helfe bei anderen Sachen anzuziehen, ich achte auch drauf, dass wenn sie irgendwohin hingeht, ich gucke was sie anzieht. Sie war sehr sauber und ordentlich. und jetzt muss ich wirklich dahinter sein. Das ist schon so, was sich verändert hat.

00:15:53-0 I: **Wie ist es mit ihrer Mobilität? Geht sie alleine raus?**

00:15:59-0 BI: Sie soll uns immer sagen wo sie hin geht, aber je nach dem sie sagt sie braucht Butter, und dann gehen mir gucken, es ist mal ein halbes. „Ich fahre Morgen einkaufen, ist es in Ordnung" „Ja", und dann packt sie ihr Rollator und fährt ins Dorf und holt dann Butter und alles Mögliche, was sie gar nicht braucht. Sie hat soviel Päckchen Kaffee in Kühlschrank und sagt „ich habe keine Kaffee mehr.." Und die Sachen sind jeden Tag wo anders... Jetzt macht sie ihre Blumen da vor dem Haus, da hat sie die gepflanzt, da gucke ich da immer Wasser ist, ich giess es auch nochmals selbst. Sie muss ja auch bisschen selbst machen.

00:17:30-0 I: **Wenn ihre Mutter wenn sie losgeht, dann findet sie auch zurück, also ist es nicht so, dass sie sich verläuft?**

00:17:36-3 BI: Nein, das noch nicht, sie finde zurück. Hier im Dorf alle kennen sie, also bis jetzt hat sie immer zurückgefunden. Ich bin auch mal mit ihr im Wald weiter gelaufen und dann meine sie, dann sind wir bis Killusberg gelaufen. Aber, ich habe sie im Glauben gelassen, das war ein Stück da hoch mal... Aber sonst, sie geht zu Lebensmittelhandel, da halte ich aber das Luft an, weil sie geht einfach auf der Straße. Ich sage ihr, „du musst es nicht wir fahren dich" „ich will mal aber auch alleine"

00:18:38-5 I: **Geht sie nur den Weg, den sie kennt?**

00:18:45-5 BI: Ja, also, sie geht gezielt zum Einkaufen und sie geht auch spazieren, da hat sie auch einen bestimmten Weg. Ich sage aber oft ich gehe mit dir. Und die Frau aus Auszeit läuft auch einen Stück mit ihr, da bin ich beruhigt da passt sie auf. Sie soll sagen wenn sie weggeht, aber sie macht es halt nicht immer. Sie wohnt unten und ich hier oben, und wir hatten so eine Schelle ein billig Teil aus Aldi, konnte sie drauf drucken und würde ich es hier oben wissen und ging unter. Sie kann schlecht laufen, ich brauche etwas was mir bemerkbar mach, dass sie mich jetzt braucht, dann kann schnell runter laufen. Weil ich gehe abends gucken, wann ist sie ins Bett, wann soll ich Strupfe ausziehen. Und morgens höre ich es auch nicht immer, wenn sie aufsteht. Dann gehe ich runter und gucke, ob sie schon soweit ist. Mit Telefonnummer weiß sie nicht mehr, manchmal weiß sie es, meistens aber nicht, da ist es so ein Zettel mit unser Nummer. Oder ich gebe ihr so oft Nummer meiner Kinder, aber dann hat sie es auch nicht mehr. Und früher wäre es nicht vorgekommen. Aber gut sie ist 92 dann.. ja, es ist... dass sie so lange gekonnt hat. Sie war eine sehr aktive Frau. Ich habe keine Ruhe, man kann sie nicht sich selbst überlassen.

00:21:25-5 I: **Seit wann wohnen Sie zusammen in der Konstellation?**

00:21:35-0 BI: Seit 1971, 40 Jahre im Dezember. Aber das hat immer gut gegangen, ich konnte dadurch wieder arbeiten gehen und wenn die Kinder von der Schule waren, sie war da. Ich war Kauffrau. Na, gut da hatte man nicht viel Möglichkeiten nach dem Krieg. Ich sollte auf höhere Schule gehen, hätte auch das geschafft aber ich hatte noch 3 Stiefschwestern, die es nicht geschafft haben. Und dann habe ich drauf konzentriert, dass meine Kinder nicht faul in der Schule waren. Meine Tochter arbeitet bei ZDF, sie ist eine Redakteurin bei 3Sat, die hat Glück gehabt. Und ja 2 Studien bezahlt... Kirsten hat in Irland dann in Berlin studiert, dann war er hier in Siegen, weil 2 Außerwertsstudiengenge ginge nicht, dann war er 3 Jahre in Australien, als er wieder kam, macht er alles anders als Architektur...

00:27:15-6 I: **Gespräch mit Demenzerkrankten**

00:30:11-1 DI: Trifft Sie es auch zu, dass manchmal so eine Sorge haben, dass Sie Unterwegs Hilfe benötigen könnten?

00:30:22-6 DI: Ja ich habe ja so ein Wagen, der mich Stützen kann, da laufe ich mit.

00:30:36-4 I: **Das gibt Ihnen Sicherheit?**

00:30:37-5 DI: Ohne dieser Wagen da könnte ich nicht mehr laufen, also mit diesem Wagen kann ich laufen. Da fühle ich mich auch sicher. Da gehe ich schon einkaufen, meistens besorgen mir das Nötigste meine Kinder, aber wenn ich z.B. zu Bäcker will, das ist nicht weit, da kann ich alleine gehen. Ich gehe meistens jeden Tag eine Runde spazieren, damit man im Bewegung bleibt.

00:31:24-9 I: **Haben Sie eine feste Runde, die Sie gehen?**

00:31:30-0 DI: Ja. Für eine Stunde bin ich weg.

00:32:00-0 I: **Wann gehen Sie Vormittags oder Nachmittags?**

00:32:03-4 DI: Nachmittags. Besorge ich mich auch schon was, was ich nötig brauche, dass ich das alleine erledigen kann, aber meistens helfen mir meine Kinder. Ich mache einen Zettel und wird dann eingekauft. Und sonst für die Wohnung da habe ich ein mal die Woche eine Hilfe, die kommt, denn ich wollte meine Tochter, damit noch belassen, die hat auch ohnehin zu tun, weil sie noch den Garten jetzt, denn ich sonst gemacht habe, noch machen muss. Und sonst hatte auch vieles zu erledigen.

00:33:02-6 I: **Und da versuchen Sie Ihre Tochter möglichst zu entlasten?**

00:33:06-9 DI: Ja

00:33:17-2 I: **Würden Sie uns noch bisschen von Ihrem Alltag erzählen, wie so ein typischer Tagesablauf von Ihnen ist?**

00:33:35-2 DI: Ich habe mein Zeit meistens, zwischen 7 und 8 stehe ich auf und mache ich mir Frühstück und dann überlege ich mir, ob ich etwas einkaufen muss, aber meistens fragt Schwiegersohn, ob ich was brauche, wenn er irgendwohin will und dann bringt er mir das mit, aber sonst gehe ich auch sehr gerne zu Geschäft, was hier unten ist im Dorf, da kann ich auch schon mal selber was erledigen.

00:34:21-0 I: **Wie wichtig ist Ihnen was selber zu erledigen?**

00:34:25-5 DI: Man will ja selbst gucken, was da angeboten wird und so, oder was günstig ist zum Einkaufen und sonst, wenn irgendwas ist, dann Helfen mir die Kinder, meine Tochter mein Schwiegersohn

00:34:54-0 I: **Gehen Sie auch Vormittags zum Einkaufen?**

00:34:57-0 DI: *Auch aber meistens Nachmittag.*

00:35:00-9 I: **Und dann Mittags mache Sie Mittagessen?**

00:35:02-9 DI: *Ja, und dann lege ich mich eine Stunde hin. Und dann, wenn ein schönes Wetter ist gehe ich raus aber sonst habe ich ein Strickzeug. Stricke Socken. Ich habe auch früher Pullover gestrickt für ein Geschäft, da wohnte ich noch in DDR und da gab es keine Witwenrente, da muss man selber gucken, wie man zurechtkommt.*

00:35:59-1 I: **Haben Sie dann konkreten Auftrag bekommen über Größe, Farbe?**

00:36:03-2 DI: *Ja, Pullover und so was.. und dann ging schon mal von hier aus rüber gefahren und habe Bekannte besucht und da bin ich an das Geschäft gegangen und da haben sie gesagt „Sie fehlen uns sehr. Das was Sie gemacht haben war immer so ordentlich und jetzt haben wir kein Nachwuchs mehr, der das sonst macht", so.. Die waren sehr aufgelöst, dass aufkehrt habe aber ich war ja nach Westen gegangen, denn dort hatte ich sehr viele Freunde Bekannte, mit denen wir heute auch in Verbindung sind, aber meine Freundin ist früh gestorben, aber trotzdem haben wir mit Kindern noch Verbindung. Wir sind jetzt noch in Verbindung. Es sind zwar schon paar Todesfälle, die man vorher kannte, das ist ja normal, aber sonst haben wir Verbindung. Jetzt geht den auch besser, weil jetzt einheitlich ist. Sie haben auch Landwirtschaft, also hungern brauchten sie nicht, aber ich bin da auch unterstützt wurde, weil waren Vertrieben und alles im Stich lassen müssen und die Dame war ein Jahr älter und wir haben uns unterstützt. Und wenn wir hier wandern, konnten wir das wieder gut machen und ihnen schicken, was sie dort nicht bekommen. die haben uns auch hier besucht und werden uns wieder besuchen. Wir rufen uns an. Wenn Geburtstag ist manchmal schreibe ich auf. Die Freundin ist seit 2 Jahren gestorben, die Kinder Leben und die Verbindung ist noch da.*

00:40:52-0 I: **Was sind aus Ihrem Sicht die größten Probleme, wenn man älter wird? Was ist es für Sie?**

00:41:30-1 DI: *Da muss ich damit abfinden, da macht man das, was man noch kann oder meine Kinder helfen mir auch, wenn ich irgendwohin will, also da habe ich keine Sorgen.*

00:41:54-1 BI: *Aber ich höre so allgemein von Altern, will ich habe noch den Kontakt zu meinem früheren Scheff, die sagen es ist sehr schwer zu akzeptieren, dass man gewisse Dinge nicht mehr kann, also ich meine Mann z.B. kann auch vieles nicht mehr, aber da sagen wir auch, wir schauen nicht zu Dem was wir nicht mehr können, wir schauen zu Dem, was wir noch können, weil andere bringt nichts. Und das höre ich von viele Älteren, da kann man dies und jenes nicht mehr und das zu akzeptieren für Leute, die viel gemacht haben, das glaube ich... das habe ich von vielen gehört, weil viele ich habe bei VDK viele Alte besucht. Die sagten das ist nicht so einfach hinzunehmen, dass man die Sachen, die man immer gemacht hat, nicht mehr kann*

00:43:10-5 I: **Darf ich fragen, ob das bei Ihnen auch so bisschen in die Richtung geht?**

00:43:17-2 DI: *Ja. Muss man sich abfinden damit, aber im Großen bin ich zufrieden. Ich kann mich noch bewegen die Sachen verschlimmern sich.. Ich bin immer in Bewegung gewesen. Meine Schwiegereltern hatten Erdbeerplantage und Landwirtschaft, da habe ich viel arbeiten müssen. Meine Eltern, die haben geschäftlich zu tun gehabt, bin ich meinem Auto gefahren und habe auch viel mitgeholfen. Ich hatte* noch einem Bruder, der ist leider gefallen im Kriegen.. und wenn er weg war müssten wir, also helfen, wenn es nur die Kaninchen zu futtern war oder Hühner.. Von Kind ab haben wir schon die Aufgaben, die man zu machen hatte. Und mein Bruder lief meistens weg zu seinen Freunden und ich war die Dumme. Ich musste schon früh schon Strümpfe stricken und so was machen... Meine Schwiegereltern hatten Erdbeerplantage und Landwirtschaft, da war auch morgens um 4 Uhr fange an zu flippen.. da mussten die geliefert werden nach Breslau. Wir hatten so einem bestimmten Händler, die das alles uns abnahmen und dann können wir zurückfahren. Wir hatten so noch 5 Kühe, die mussten ja gemolken werden - das musste ich auch schon früh machen..

00:48:18-5 I: **Wie weit war es?**

00:48:20-5 DI: *30km 35km, mit Auto(Lieferwagen) Wenn di markt anfing da, muss alles da sein, kriegen Geld dafür wir hatten unsere bestimmten Abnehmer, die mussten ja dann um 6 Uhr anfangen. Ich habe auch selber dahingefahren, ich hatte den Führerschein. Und wegen Vertreibung dürften wir nichts mitnehmen, gar nichts mehr... es war schlimm. Mein man war noch gefallen. Ich hatte noch den Freund von meinem Mann, dem starb die Frau und dann habe ich noch mal geheiratet. Drüben gab es keine Witwenrente in der DDR, kriegst du nichts, muss du sehen wie mann zurechtkam, bei der Vertreibung konnte man nur das mitnehmen, was man noch tragen konnte. Ich hatte damals in der Nähe von Dresden hatten, wo wir einquartiere waren, freundliche Leute gefunden, mit denen wir noch in Verbindung sind. Es war schon schlimme Zeit, aber hatten da Glück gehabt, dass wir gute Leute hatten, die uns aufgenommen haben*

00:53:03-0 I: **Wie sind Sie in Siegener Raum gelandet?**

00:53:10-3 BI: *Ihr Mann wohnte hier.*

00:53:21-0 DI: *Mein zweiter Mann Freund meines ersten Mannes. Und da hatte er in Post seiner Frau meine Adresse gefunden. Und da hatte er mir geschrieben und hatte gefragt, ob ich nicht hierüber kommen möchte. ich sagte, dass ich es mir noch über legen muss, aber dann komme ich doch zu den Entschluss, die Leute in DDR waren zwar nett, man kriegte keine Rente, hier konnte ich dann Witwenrente beantragen. Und die Kinder meines Mannes kannten mich schon, die waren 3 Kinder und meine Tochter, sie war dann die Jüngste, wir haben noch heute gutes Verhältnis. Ich hatte die Kleidung genäht, aber jetzt nicht mehr...*

01:00:59-4 I: **(System erklärt) Wie schätzen Sie so was ein?**

01:01:03-8 DI: *Eigentlich bis jetzt bin ich zurechtgekommen*

01:01:09-3 BI: *Wenn sie irgendwo in Kreuztal ist, sind wir auch dabei, aber ich konnte es mir auch vorstellen, das es eine Hilfe ist, wenn man so was hat, ich bin schon auch 70. Wenn wir z.B. Köln sind, da kenne ich mich nicht aus, gut ich kann fragen, aber das wäre schon nicht schlecht.*

01:01:44-4 I: **(Überwachung) Wie würden Sie das einschätzen, was Privatsphäre Aspekt angeht?**

01:02:58-8 DI: *Ja, ich meine hier bin ich bekannt und finde mich noch zurecht. Alleine fahre ich nie weg, also da ist immer jemand dabei. Das ist deswegen für mich nicht so notwendig*

01:05:07-7 BI: *(bezüglich Überwachung) Das kann man nicht ganz ausschließen, man muss ja immer gucken, ob alles in Ordnung ist und ich finde solche Sensoren, weil für die, die alleine lebt, finde ich es nicht schlecht finden. Wenn meine Mutter noch in Kreuztal noch alleine lebte, dann wäre es mir Hilfe, wenn ich kontrollieren konnte, ob irgendwas jetzt nicht in Ordnung ist. Ja das ist eine gewisse Sache von Kontrolle, die aber dann sein muss, wenn ein Mensch so alt ist und es wird mit Alter nicht besser. Oder kommt die Diakonie ich hatte eine Freundin, Altenpflegerin, die gingen auch 1-2 Mal in solche ... und wenn etwas nicht stimmt die haben Schlüssel und kommen darein und so... aber so was ist natürlich auch eine Hilfe. Wenn Einer keine Diakonie braucht, dann kommt nicht unbedingt jemand.*

01:06:20-7 DI: *Ich habe ja gegenüber eine Nachbarin, die nachguckt, wenn meine Tochter und mein Schwiegersohn weg sind.*

01:06:37-4 I: **Das finden Sie gut, dass es so ist?**

01:06:38-5 DI: *Ja. Und die anderen Nachbarn geben Acht*

01:06:44-5 BI: *Alle alarmiert, wenn wir Fahren*

01:06:54-2 I: **Wie würden Sie diesen Aspekt „Kontrolle" einschätzen?**

01:07:15-6 DI: *Meine Tochter kommt auch runter und fragt „ist alles in Ordnung?"*

01:07:23-5 I: **Das ist auch für Sie in Ordnung?**

01:07:25-3 DI: *Ja, ja. Die Nachbarin ist Krankenpflegerin (Altenpflegerin), die guckt auch nach mir. Da brauche ich keine Angst zu haben oder Sorgen.*

E. Interview transcript D (German)

Interview mit dem Demenzkranken und dessen Betreuer

I - Interviewer
DI - Dementer Interviewpartner
BI - Betreuender Interviewpartner
PI - Pflegende Interviewpartner

Kreuztal, den 26.06.2011

Interviewtranskript

00:00:25-9 I: *Es ist ein schweres Feld, wie haben Sie damit umgegangen?*

00:00:35-7 BI: *Ich muss es lernen. Ich gehe ein mal im Monat, Selbsthilfegruppe für Demenzkrankenangehörige hier in Kreuztal, bei der Diakonie und jetzt haben wir zusammengetan mit diese einem Heim, die haben Demenzkrankewohngemeinschaft, und deren Angehörige ich habe mit denen zusammengetroffen und dann haben wir so ein Film angeschaut „Eines Tages" - sehr Lehrreich also drei Familien die mit Demenz umgehen. Es geht um MutterßTochter verhältnis und ich habe mich teilweise drin gesehen. sie geht ruppig mit Mutter um und die Mutter nervt auch richtig, meine Schwigermutter ist auch sehr böse, lässt sich nicht sagen und dominante Frau, Sie war eine dominante Frau gewesen und immer herrig und bestimmend und ich als Schwiegertochter mache 99% - versorge sie. Einerseits ist sie froh drauf aber andererseits passt ihr vieles nicht, wenn ich ihr sage „es fleck drauf" - „was du von mir alles siehst, alles ist sauber, brauchst keine Sorgen zu machen". Und sie ist sparsam, wenn ich eine sparsame Antwort gebe, dann geht das. Und so zu reden erfahre ich in Selbsthilfegruppen. Ich kenne paar Leute, die schon 5ß6 Jahre dabei sind und die sagen es ist ganz ganz langsamer Lernprozess für die Angehörige, wie man reagiert, manchmal nervt es, mache Tage ist man hoch drauf, manche Tage kann man nichts vertragen. Und manchmal kommt sie sagt eine Wort und man hat schone eine schlechte Laune. Und wenn ich ihr sage, was ist denn wieder los? dann sagt sie „ist mir schlecht" „ich habe schlecht geschlafen", aber vorher vor 2 Stunden hat sie gesagt „ich habe wunderbar geschlafen". Wenn sie sich in die Ecke*

97

getrieben fühlt, sagt sie „ich habe schlecht geschlafen". Das ist ein Begründungsmüster. Sie weisst dass irgendwas nicht stimmt, wenn ich sage „was ich falsch gemacht habe? ich wollte dir nur helfen", dann merkt sie ich wollte wirklich helfen und dann sagt sie ich habe schlecht geschlafen.

00:04:40-8 I: **Wie erklären Sie sich diese Stimmungsschwankungen so stark sind?**

00:04:57-7 BI: Ich weiss es nicht ich muss das noch rausfinden. Sie trinkt manchmal nicht und die wenig Trinker sind oft durcheinander. Wir habe selber eine Firma, da muss ich auch in die Firma.

00:06:30-6 I: **Lebt noch Schwiegervater auch?**

00:06:32-6 BI: Nein, der ist seit 1997 Tod. Sie ist 87, sie will das nicht Wahr haben. Seit 81 habe ich gemerkt, dass ihr schlechter geht, seitdem merke ich die Veränderung. In letztem Jahr hatte in Krankenhaus gewesen, weil sie Schwindel hatte und ihr war schlecht und da haben die alles untersucht und festgestellt das sie Demenzkrank(02.2010) ist und da war sie richtig, richtig böse. Sie hat Demenz nicht Alzheimer im Anfang wenn sie merkte das sie helle Momente hat. Ihre Schwester hat kein Demenz, aber glaube Alteschemie , aber wenn sie etwas vergisst dann lacht sie einfach. Sie gibt nichts zu, dann wird sie böse und versucht das anderen zu schieben. Du hast mir das nicht gesagt

00:08:46-1 I: **Können sie noch nach ersten Zeichen erinnern, wo sie gemerkt haben etwas stimmt nicht?**

00:09:00-4 BI: Mit saubermachen mit dem Kochen. Letztes Jahr im August, wo es noch akut war, da haben ganze Verwandten gedacht, sie hat allen rum angerufen, sagte dass wir sie quälen, was wir alle mit ihr machen. Und die haben ins zurückgerufen was ist los, und die haben sie mit genommen, weil wir sie so schlecht behandeln. Dann habe ich letztes Jahr gesagt, ab jetzt, sie hat mit Zug gefahren überall nach Stuttgart oder nach Berlin, und die haben sie abgeholt. Sie hat umgestiegen in Hagen oder in Frankfurt. Ich sagte das geht nicht mehr, wenn sie sie haben möchten, möchten sie auch hier abholen und hier abliefern. Und im Letzten August war dieser Durcheinander. Sie haben sie in den Zug gesetzt und von Stuttgart nach Berlin geschickt und im Berlin sagte sie wollte nach Hause. Und wir holten sie im Hagen, das können wir nicht wir sind alle beschäftigt. Mein Mann sagte, ich war nicht da, sie wusste nicht wo sie war, mein Hausarzt sagte mir es ist Glück das sie ausgestiegen ist, sie könne irgendwo aussteigen können. Und dann war sie zu Hause und wollte sie sich was kochen. Ich koche für sie aber paar Tage war ich nicht da. Da war sie am Reise kochen ohne Wasser. Das hat gedauert bis sie gemerkt hat dass sie in ihrer alter Umgebung ist. Das hat sie total verwirrt. Und wenn Angehörigen kommen - sie freut sich, aber es ist ungewohnte Situation. Sie ist damit überfordert. Sie sagt nichts aber ich merke eine Woche... Sie hat 4 Kinder(3 Söhne, Tochter - 3. Kind). Diese Wetter Schwankungen, ob sie es trinkt genug... ich bin um 12 weg, ich sage ihr, dass sie Trinken muss, dann wird sie böse... Sie sagt ich habe alles immer gemacht, wird sie böse... sie hatte am Anfang 80 Jahre an einem Auge Infarkt und da konnte sie ganz schlecht sehen und jetzt kann sie ganz schlecht sehen, dann wird sie schmutzige Sachen in den Schrank tun.

00:15:44-4 I: **Und diese Frau aus Auszeit, kann sie sagen, dass es ist nicht richtig sauber?**

00:15:56-1 BI: Wir haben gesagt, dass sie mehr als angenehmer Partnerin sein soll, sie macht alles auf ganz tolle Art. Das hat viel gedauert, bis sie sie akzeptiert hat... Sie hat immer geguckt, wo sie was gerne macht und sie hat immer gerne gebacken, und dann hat die Frau Kämpfer Nussecken zu machen, hat sie auch etwas machen können. Das hat paar Monate gedauert, bis sie akzeptiert hat. Und jetzt wenn sie nicht kommt dann vermisst sie sie. Es gibt so ein buch von NRW für Demenzkranke, wie man die so beschäftigen kann, das hat geholfen, sie fang an zu erzählen, wie war die Kindheit und wir haben das alles ausgeschrieben und Alben gemacht und wir haben in alten Alben gesucht die passend zu diesen Geschichten waren. Ich versuche immer die Diskussion zu vermeiden, weil sie wird schnell böse. Dauernd habe ich Konfrontation mit ihr, wenn ich ihre Sachen wasche, wird sie böse „was war wieder schmutzig"

00:25:55-5 I: *Ist sie auch so mit Ihrem Sohn?*

00:26:00-0 BI: *Nein, deswegen muss ich paar Sachen über ihm sagen lassen, z.B. beim Duschen sie geht auch nicht... Sie sagte ich habe heute geduscht, ich sagte nein das war nicht heute... Und da muss ich bisschen drohen, ich sagte wenn du nicht duschst muss ich Krankenkasse anrufen und die schicken jemandem der dich duscht, sie war sehr böse, sie sagte „du unterstehst dich", aber seitdem 3 bis 4 mal duschen, ab und zu muss man bisschen drohen... Zu Sohn ist sie ganz anders, was sie mir sagt sie ihm im anderem Tone oder gar nicht. Sie hat nicht vertragen, wenn mein Mann meiner Meinung war und wird böse. Sie dusch alleine, noch... Baden-Wiesborn sie kannte sich aus in diesem Haus, aber leider dieses Haus pleite gegangen... Jetzt wollte ich nicht in ein Fremdes tun... sie kannte alles da... Sie ist 2 mal in der Woche in Tagespflege(um 8 wird sie geholt und bis 16 - sie ist unheimlich gerne dort) und 2 mal der Woche kommt Frau Kämpfer aus Auszeit(3 Stunden). Sie geht sehr gerne dahin, wir haben Glück damit. Sie haben helle Räume ein Garten, sie ist sehr gerne da(Tagespflege Freudenberg) In einem Jahr ihr Zustand ist sehr verschlechtert. Die Demenz ist vielfältig, anstrengend und man ist sehr gebunden. Ich muss für sie kochen, muss sehen, dass sie duscht, und dann liegen diese Gegenstände überall.*

00:39:17-0 I: *Wie oft kochen sie für Ihre Schwiegermutter?*

00:39:22-9 BI: *Ich bringe es rüber, mit Mikrowelle klappt es noch... Montags, Dienstags, Donnerstags, Samstags, Sonntags zwei Tage ist sie in Tagespflege... Ich habe Putzfrau engagiert, aber Schwiegermutter sagt „sie brauch nicht zu kommen alles sauber..."*

00:45:14-4 I: *Wenn die Frau Kämpfer geht dann ist Ihre Schwiegermutter alleine, aber kriegt ihrem tag organisiert?*

00:45:25-4 BI: *Ja,.. organisiert - sie weiss nicht, was sie machen soll... was die Demenzkranken machen, die sortieren wieder... Sie hat ihrem Mann teilweise nicht erkannt, und ich habe ihr gesagt „du hast ja so tolle Geschichten erzählt". Sie haben 1950 verheiratet. Alles was bis Krieg war - das kriegt sie noch hin, aber später nicht mehr.*

00:48:22-1 I: *Help-Yourself?*

00:48:53-1 BI: *Das finde ich für tolle Idee, aber sie kommt allein mit Fernbedienung nicht zu Recht*

00:49:02-7 I: *Wegen Krankheit oder Alter?*

00:49:06-4 BI: *Wegen Krankheit*

00:55:44-1 I: *Geht Ihre Schwiegermutter raus?*

00:55:47-4 BI: *Ja, bis jetzt war sie sehr beweglich, aber ich habe seit paar Wochen bemerkt sie hat wenig Lust zu gehen, aber sonst sie läuft ganzen Tal rum, sie geht bis zum nächsten Dorf und das ist ganz ein ganz schönes Stück. Sie ist mit Rollator*

00:56:35-1 I: *Sie findet aber wieder zurück?*

00:56:39-9 BI: *Nein hier nicht, sie ist hier geboren hier zur Schule gegangen, das kennt sie alles von Früher, auch nächste Dörfchen, noch nie passiert... Sie hat bis 80 Fahrrad gefahren. Die Charakter verstärkt sich mit der Demenz.*

01:01:50-4 I: *Wie würden Sie sich vorstellen, für sich technische Hilfe in Anspruch zu nehmen?*

01:02:09-4 BI: *Jetzt wenn ich klar im Verstand bin - Ja. Ich denke meine Generation oder jüngere, die mit Technik zu tun haben die Leben damit, die werden später keine Probleme damit haben. Sie kennt sich mit Technik gar nicht aus. Jemand hat mir gesagt es gibt so eine kette, wo man mit irgendeine ... GPS ortet, die werden aber das nicht in de Reihe kriegen.*

01:03:16-6 I: *Wie würden Sie so ein Technik unter dem Geschichtspunkt Privatheit Autonomie?*

01:03:20-0 BI: *Ich finde es in dem Zustand gut. Als besser wenn sie sich Gott weiss... Und wenn sie wissen gar nicht, wo sie sind, das merken die. Das finde ich gut. Ich habe das erstmal gestern gehörte, ich war in der Altenheim, sie geht gerne spazieren, die haben mir gesagt, dann tuen wir so ein Ding, aber sie muss etwas drucken das geht nicht, das wird sie nicht finden, sie sagten dann können wir Orten, wo sie ist das wusste ich nicht, wenn sie in fremden Gegend ist. Das finde ich toll, so ein Ding, ich finde es ist kein Eingriff in die Privatsphäre. Ich glaube in dem Zustand ist es sehr hilfreich. Ihre Freundin, sie kann sich nicht so viel Bewegen, aber sie ist ganz klar im Kopf, und sie ist allein im Haus, ihr Sohn geht arbeiten, sie hat so ein Dingen, sie tut es sofort drauf... sie würde das annehmen, ich finde es ist eine Hilfe... Ich merke ab und zu, dass sie merk, dass sie vieles nicht kann und das sie vieles nicht behält, auch vieles nicht weiss, und jetzt ist sie alleine da...*

01:23:37-2 I: *Vielleicht sollen wir das nicht Hilfe Tool nennen, weil sie es nicht akzeptieren*

01:23:40-2 BI: *Ja, ja das stimmt, das finde ich toll. Weil viele wollen einkaufen gehen, was sie einkaufen ist teilweise unwichtig, aber das Gefühl einkaufen zu gehen. Aber das Einkaufszentrum kennt sie nicht mehr, sie kannte ein altes Lädchen, aber es ist nicht mehr da und das ist das Problem, aber sie will es selbständig zu machen.. Sie kennen alles von Früher aber neues sie kennen es nicht.*

01:26:13-2 I: *Wen auch das wiederholt wird?*

01:26:15-0 BI: *Nein das wird nichts bringen.*

00:02:55-4 I: *Ihre Schwiegertochter hat uns erzählt, dass sie so eine grosse Landwirtschaft hatten? Dass Sie so eine tüchtige Frau sind.*

00:03:03-7 DI: *Bin ich von langem früher und ich habe viele Kinder und die Eltern habe ich noch gepflegt, demenzkrank waren Die, zwei Jahre. Dann musste ich meinem Mann noch hergeben - das ist aller schlimmste.*

00:04:00-8 I: *Demenzkranke haben oft innere Unruhen, laufen ganz viel, war es auch bei Ihrem Eltern auch so?*

00:04:08-5 DI: *Erste Zeit mein Vater wollte immer weg, dann habe ich alle Türen geschlossen dass er im Bett bleiben muss oder oben bleiben musste. Ich musste drauf und unter... Letzte Nacht sagte meine Stiefmutter „Nach Hana" Dann hat er gestorben. Er ging in Fenster und ruf Hilfe und dann habe ich alle Fenster und Türen alles festzumachen, weil er nicht raus und rufen konnte.*

00:05:42-3 I: *Jetzt gibt es z.B. Geräte , womit man orten kann, wo sich eine oder derjenige Person befindet.*

00:05:58-1 DI: *So was gab es früher nicht.*

00:06:15-2 PI: *Man muss Technik beherrschen, aber dann weiss man, wo man seinen lieben Menschen wieder findet.*

00:06:25-0 DI: *Da hatte ich kein Zeit hinterherzulaufen, ich hatte keine Zeit zu (1977)*

00:07:10-5 PI: *Auf heutige Zeit könnte man Eltern allein spazieren gehen lassen..*

00:07:18-5 DI: *Nein, alleine auf keinen Fall, sie sind so vertritt, und sie wissen nicht, wo sie sind. Deshalb habe ich alles zugeschlossen. Ich kann keinem so eine Krankheit im Haus.*

00:09:10-0 I: *Waren Ihre Eltern schon alt?*

00:09:14-9 BI: *Ja Vater war 87 und Mutter 85. Aber sie war sehr beweglich, aber sie begriff nicht, dass sie im Bett liegen musste.*

00:10:16-6 I: *Hatten Sie auch Hilfe bei der Pflege Ihrer Eltern?*

00:10:22-2 DI: *Geschwistern war alle beide weg, ich war immer alleine*

00:11:39-0 I: *War so, dass Ihre Haushalt relativ getrennt waren?*

00:11:52-5 DI: *Nein, wir waren immer zusammen*

00:23:16-3 I: *(System erklärt)*

00:26:24-8 DI: *Das werde ich aber brauchen können.*

00:24:03-3 BI: *Akustisch, gut... Grünen Knopf damit sie das sehen können.*

00:26:24-8 DI: *Es ist nicht einfach demenzkrank zu leben*

00:28:18-2 BI: *Sie beschwert, dass sie nicht mehr Fahrrad fahren kann.*

00:28:22-0 DI: *Darf! Mein Sohn hat mir gesagt, untersteh dich den Fahrrad zu nehmen. Früher habe ich immer mit Fahrrad gefahren. Jetzt habe ich jemandem, der mir etwas immer mitbringt, obwohl manchmal wollte ich etwas selber einkaufen wollte, nach Kreuztal und gucken über alles.*

00:29:23-9 BI: *Habe ich auch das gesagt, alles wo du hingegangen bist, ist weg*

00:29:34-4 DI: *Und überhaupt andere Leute zu sehen, aber alleine will ich das.*

00:29:43-4 I: *Warum ist das so wichtig?*

00:29:46-0 DI: *Ja, dass ich erzählen und hören kann.*

00:29:52-0 BI: *Ohne Zuhörer. Ein mal im Monat geht sie in so ein Altenkreis. Das ist sehr wichtig*

00:30:33-6 DI: *Nur schade meine beste Kusine, sie hat mich überall mitgenommen, sie hat ... Jahr gestorben. Wir haben aber schönes Zeit zusammen gehabt, dann war sie krank, ich habe ihr Essen gebracht. Sie hatte schmerzen am Bein. Wir habe auch verschiedene Spiele gespielt*

00:35:00-0 I: *Spielen Sie jetzt auch?*

00:35:01-0 DI: *Ja, wenn ich jemandem dabei habe..*

F. Content analysis by Mayring (German)

- **Z1: Paraphrasierung**

  - Z1.1: Streiche alle nicht (oder wenig) inhaltstragenden Textbestandteile wie ausschmückende, wiederholende, verdeutlichende Wendungen!

  - Z1.2: Übersetze die inhaltstragenden Textstellen auf eine einheitliche Sprachebene!

  - Z1.3: Transformiere sie auf eine grammatikalische Kurzform!

- **Z2: Generalisierung auf das Abstraktionsniveau**

  - Z2.1: Generalisiere die Gegenstände der Paraphrasen auf die definierte Abstraktionsebene, sodass die alten Gegenstände in den neu formulierten impliziert sind!

  - Z2.2: Generalisiere die Satzaussagen (Prädikate) auf die gleiche Weise!

  - Z2.3: Belasse die Paraphrasen, die über dem angestrebten Abstraktionsniveau liegen!

  - Z2.4: Nimm theoretische Vorannahmen bei Zweifelsfällen zuhilfe!

- **Z3: Erste Reduktion**

  - Z3.1: Streiche bedeutungsgleiche Paraphrasen innerhalb der Auswertungseinheiten!

  - Z3.2: Streiche Paraphrasen, die auf dem neuen Abstraktionsniveau nicht als wesentlich inhaltstragend erachtet werden!

  - Z3.3: Übernehme die Paraphrasen, die weiterhin als zentral inhaltstragend erachtet werden (Selektion)!

  - Z3.4: Nimm theoretische Vorannahmen bei Zweifelsfällen zuhilfe!

- **Z4: Zweite Reduktion**

  - Z4.1: Fasse Paraphrasen mit gleichem (ähnlichem) Gegenstand und ähnlicher Aussage zu einer Paraphrase (Bündelung) zusammen!

  - Z4.2: Fasse Paraphrasen mit mehreren Aussagen zu einem Gegenstand zusammen (Konstruktion/Integration)!

  - Z4.3: Fasse Paraphrasen mit gleichem (ähnlichem) Gegenstand und verschiedener Aussage zu einer Paraphrase zusammen (Konstruktion/Integration)!

  - Z4.4 Nimm theoretische Vorannahmen bei Zweifelsfällen zuhilfe!